STAKIS

THE REO STAKIS STORY

Other books by Jack Webster:

THE DONS

GORDON STRACHAN

'TIS BETTER TO TRAVEL

ALISTAIR MACLEAN: A LIFE

FAMOUS SHIPS OF THE CLYDE

THE FLYING SCOTS

GRAINS OF TRUTH

THE EXPRESS YEARS

IN THE DRIVING SEAT

THE HERALD YEARS

WEBSTER'S WORLD

FROM DALI TO BURRELL

STAKIS

THE REO STAKIS STORY

JACK WEBSTER

First published 1999
by B&W Publishing Ltd, Edinburgh
ISBN 1 873631 97 9
Copyright © Jack Webster 1999

The right of Jack Webster to be identified as
author of this work has been asserted by him
in accordance with the Copyright, Designs
and Patents Act 1988.

British Library Cataloguing in Publication Data:
A catalogue record for this book is available
from the British Library.

Photographs of Crawfordjohn, the Grosvenor and Andros Stakis
courtesy of The Herald Picture Archive

Cover design: Winfortune & Associates

Printed by WSOY

CONTENTS

ACKNOWLEDGEMENTS

My thanks to the many dozens of witnesses who enabled me to reach a clearer understanding of Sir Reo Stakis. Special credit goes to his long-standing secretary, Frances Timoney, and to the Director of Communications at the Stakis organisation, Alex Pagett.

J. W.

PROLOGUE

DAY OF DRAMA

On a grey day in February 1999 cars were streaming into the grounds of the stately Stakis Dunblane Hotel in Perthshire for a gathering at which human emotion would run high.

There had never been a turnout like this before but, then again, there had never been the prospect—by now a near-certainty—that these people would be attending the very last annual general meeting of the great Stakis organisation.

They were mainly private shareholders and 800 of them had come to have their final say on the takeover bid which now lay before them. The predator was that old rival, the Ladbroke Group, owners of Hilton International, which was about to swallow up Stakis and not only remove yet another quoted company from its Scottish roots but bring to an end one of the legendary tales of business romance.

The creator and central figure of that romance, Sir Reo Stakis, came quietly upon the scene that day, walking with Lady Stakis and other members of the family from their home in the grounds of what was formerly known as the Dunblane Hydro.

They arrived to a bustle of mounting anticipation in the foyer as shareholders began to file into the meeting, which extended to an overflow audience linked up by closed-circuit television.

Clearly, those investors were there for a fight, caring less for the

1

bumper benefits they were due to reap from the Ladbroke offer than for the fact that, ironically in these final weeks of the run-in towards a devolved parliament in Edinburgh, the Scottish people were about to lose one of their favourite companies.

Not least, their feelings were for the 86-year-old Reo Stakis himself, a man they admired and respected and who would certainly not have chosen such a fate as this for his life's work. He made that patently clear in a brief address, in which he recalled that he had come to this country as a young boy from Cyprus to sell his mother's lace and was proud that he had built up an enterprise of hotels, restaurants and casinos which employed 14,500 people.

The true depth of his heartache could only be guessed by the vast gathering which gave him a thunderous reception. The general mood was one of criticism and regret that the company was being delivered into the hands of Ladbroke.

Paradoxically, the man widely credited with having rescued Stakis from the doldrums of 1990, chief executive David Michels, became the main target of attack. If the takeover went through, the London-born Mr Michels was being lined up as chief executive of the entire Hilton International, where he had been an executive vice-president before taking over the Stakis position. In the modern manner, he would also be much the richer from share options.

For all the fire and fury, however, private shareholders had to face the harsh reality that there is little room for sentiment in business and that money most decidedly talks louder than words. The plain fact was that Michels and his team had rebuilt a hotel and leisure group which had now attracted an offer of £1.2 billion.

Chairman Robert Smith and his board had no option but to recommend such an offer and the power of acceptance lay not with the loyalty of the private people but with the large and faceless institutions which held an unanswerable 87 per cent of the shares.

At least that final annual general meeting offered the chance of a farewell gesture to its founder. The entire company adjourned to the vast dining area for a buffet lunch, where Sir Reo and Lady Stakis mingled with their large circle of friends.

Four of their six children were there, elder son Andros being joined by sisters Rena from Athens, Niki from Limassol and Stassia from Los Angeles.

The formalities of Stakis being absorbed into the framework of Hilton International would be completed in the springtime, raising the number of Hilton hotels in the United Kingdom from 38 to 92, and giving them an extra 22 casinos as well as 68 health clubs of the LivingWell brand.

Turning the tables, there had been an occasion when Reo Stakis bought over a number of Ladbroke casinos; but the former boss of that enterprise, Cyril Stein, had never been one of his favourite people. Indeed he once took Stein to court to secure a settlement. So there was an element of bitter irony as he now prepared to step away from his life's creation.

But he was doing so with the dignity you could expect from the reserve of his nature and the strength of his character. At Dunblane that day, the pianist had set a scene of mellow harmony as diners exchanged reminiscences and queued up to take their farewells of the modest Cypriot who had engraved the name of Stakis in the vocabulary of his adopted land.

As far as that gathering was concerned, there would have been a rousing response if, by chance, the piano had broken into a chorus of "He's a Jolly Good Fellow."

1

WHERE IT ALL BEGAN

In the springtime of 1998, as he reached his 85th birthday, Sir Reo
Stakis went back to his native island of Cyprus on what might
have seemed like one of his regular visits. Down the years, in fact,
he had spaced those returns so that their flavour would not be
dimmed by too much familiarity and, on this occasion, he was to
recall that he had not been back in his homeland for nearly two
years.

There was, therefore, a sense of special occasion as he boarded
that Air 2000 flight at Glasgow Airport on April Fool's Day and
took his place among Scottish holidaymakers who were seeking
an early brush with the sun in the approach to Easter weekend.
There were frolicsome children in the seats around him but the
constant chatter and movement served only to bring out the warm
indulgence he had always shown to youngsters, not least his own.

They were at the beginning of their lives whereas he, in the
quieter moments of the flight, was reflecting on his own mortality.
Life did not go on for ever. Time was precious and the older you
became the more you realised the need to value every nuance of
your days and to make the most of them. In spite of heart surgery
and previous health scares, Sir Reo was in remarkably good shape,
a bundle of energy who could still walk ahead of younger friends
and set an example in keeping the body in good trim.

It was an attitude of mind which had stood him in good stead since he first left this Mediterranean paradise more than seventy years ago, a boy of barely fifteen, to start out on an adventure which would bring him fame and fortune, high points and heartaches, and turn him into the best-known living Cypriot.

In the United Kingdom, and most surely in Scotland, the name of Stakis was a household word, a symbol of hotels, restaurants, casinos and so much more which owed their existence to this remarkable little man who was born Argiros Anastasis in 1913 and decided, with good commercial sense, to shorten his name to a more manageable Reo Stakis.

As the plane came down the flight-path towards Larnaca Airport, daughter Niki and her husband Evros, who live in Cyprus, were waiting to greet him and transport him to the base for this visit, which would be the Amathus Beach hotel in Limassol.

The Amathus Beach was built by a Cypriot friend, Evagoras Lanitis, a university student in London who had gone on holiday with some friends to play tennis in Glasgow where he met Cathy, a lassie from Govan with whom he fell instantly in love. They married and returned to Cyprus, where Evagoras's father was a prominent businessman. They built the Amathus Beach, which became one of the best-known hotels on the island, and added two more to their stable before Evagoras died. Cathy from Govan was still there towards the end of the century, a prosperous widow who had become totally integrated into the Greek community of her adopted island.

Family and friends joined Sir Reo for dinner at the Amathus that evening and this pilgrimage to the homeland would begin after breakfast next morning when the chauffeur awaited the small party and set off on the first outing, which would take them high into the Troodos Mountains, with their magnificent views of this Mediterranean island.

After leaving a Scotland in the grip of unpredictable weather, the snowstorms of winter having switched their season to spring, the first surprise was to find that the Troodos slopes of Cyprus were also deep in snow. The shrine to Archbishop Makarios stands at the high point of the mountains but the immediate destination was lower down the range, at the Kikkos Monastery, where the first President of Cyprus had gained his early education on the way to priesthood.

During the drive to Kikkos, Sir Reo was struck by the fact that, for all his return visits, he had not been this particular way since 1936, when he went back home with his proud possession, a brand new Singer car, a measure of the progress he had made in his business venture in Britain. The route back to Cyprus had been by ferry to France, a long drive across Europe to Brindisi, on the heel of south-eastern Italy, and finally a boat trip to Cyprus.

On that visit of more than sixty years earlier he had packed his mother and other members of the family into the Singer car and driven them up the mountains. It was the return journey from Kikkos Monastery that day which stuck most in his memory because of a horrifying incident. As darkness fell on that steep and winding road, Reo Stakis was driving behind two cars which served to guide him on the tortuous route. The leading driver faced the oncoming headlights of another car in the belief that they were on a straight stretch of road. In fact there was a double bend between them.

Caught up in the illusion, he drove straight across the small embankment and down a ravine, to be followed by the second car which had taken its cue from the first. Reo Stakis's Singer was following exactly the same route as he suddenly realised what was happening and jammed on the brakes. His car hung perilously on the brink of disaster as he scrambled out, released members of his family and set about helping those in the ravine.

Miraculously, nobody was killed. Reo summoned help from a nearby village and saw the victims on their way to hospital. Some of those survivors owed their lives to the fact that penicillin, so recently discovered by a Scotsman, Alexander Fleming, had just reached Cyprus for the first time.

It was a drama which had remained with him all those years but now he was travelling on roads which were vastly improved from the dirt-track days, broader and with good surfaces and with signs which alerted you to those deceptive turns.

At the monastery once graced by Archbishop Makarios a priest was quick to recognise his unexpected visitor, setting a pattern which would become so familiar during this return to his homeland. It soon became clear to accompanying friends that Reo Stakis was almost certainly the best-known Cypriot beyond the island's own boundaries. If he was not recognised from appearance, the name brought an instant response wherever he went, weather-beaten faces lighting up with warmth and admiration.

He would stop off at a little village and within minutes find himself in deep conversation with an old man sitting in his doorway or an industrious lady who would pause from her lace-making to offer a welcome and gaze thoughtfully at him. In most cases they would have common acquaintances; Sir Reo would have known a grandfather or an uncle, emphasising the incredible depth of family connection and intermingling on an island like Cyprus.

In the case of the women in particular, they would strike the outsider as being old before their time, dressed in black while still in middle age, much as our grandmothers used to be in Scotland two generations earlier. They may not yet have caught up with western ways, the fashions and the fickleness, but there was a touching decency in those friendly faces, creased with the burdens of a hard but contented life.

They knew exactly who Reo Stakis was and found it hard to believe that he had chanced upon their doorstep just like that. The man was clearly a living legend in Cyprus, the local hero whose story had been passed down to children. Lady Stakis was not with

7

him on this visit. She too was so well-known and loved on the island that she sometimes found it difficult to cope with the numbers who turned up to see her on the rare returns.

But Sir Reo was determined to see again that village of Lefkara which had given him the charming girl who would become his wife. Through the winding streets he strolled, accepting greetings from every doorway and stopping to embrace old friends who would suddenly appear in front of him with arms outstretched. It was a deeply moving experience for all concerned.

That labyrinth of quaint streets would lead him to the local Greek Orthodox Church. The doors were locked but there he stood in private remembrance of that day in 1946 when he and Anna Petropoulos were married in this place. What a swell affair it had been in this handsome building, with its grandstand view of a spectacular valley, and it was here that 2000 people had gathered for the union of two much respected families from those peasant villages just two miles apart in the lower mountains of Cyprus.

The size of the guest-list shows once again the maze of family connections, everyone apparently related to everyone else and all welcome at the wedding. In fact the reception had to be split in two, one half in each village.

Now there was a special poignancy as he approached the street where his beloved Anna (or Annitsa, as he came to call her) was born and grew up. This was her village, her street, her home and the present owners came to welcome him into the house. What he had not yet noticed was that, since his last visit to Lefkara, they had renamed Annitsa's street STAKIS AVENUE. Sir Reo looked bewildered.

He joined some locals at a street café and gazed down that magnificent valley below Lefkara, remembering those courting days of the late 1930s when he came back from Britain to look for a wife. The next stop on this pilgrimage would take him back to the village where it all began in 1913, back to Kato-Drys, which had bred him and raised him and seen him on his way to a vastly different life in Britain. It was just two miles away.

2

CRISIS IN THE FAMILY

The village of Kato-Drys lies twenty-two miles inland from Larnaca, capital town of the district, and could pass at first sight for a deserted hamlet, so still and peaceful and hung with an air of melancholy, as if in remembrance of better times gone by.

Reo Stakis paused on the outskirts and looked across the dip in the land, which his father had once struggled to farm and which remained in his family possession, though there was not much you could do with a tract of ground like that in the modern economy.

Above the village rose terrace after terrace of derelict vineyard, reminiscent of a spacious forum of Roman times, where his father and dozens like him in the village had scratched a bare living in the cultivation of the grape; now they were deserted in the all-too-familiar story of the small farmer who has gone from being the salt of the earth to become an uneconomical unit in a profit-driven society. Cyprus wine is now extracted from more accessible vineyards and much of it is taken in bulk to countries like Germany.

So Sir Reo drove into Kato-Drys and straight to that little street where he was born. This had once been a community within a community, half a dozen houses which formed a neighbourhood of their own, but now they were all gone except the house of Stakis. Crumbling into decay, they had been demolished giving a different perspective to the one remaining building, which survived because Sir Reo still looked after it.

The key was held by the leader of the village, who promptly materialised with the customary welcome and unlocked the property for its owner. At first sight it might have seemed to the stranger a house larger than you would expect, until you remembered that this was not just the dwelling-place of the family but virtually the farmyard as well, gathering-point for the produce of the fields—and home for the donkeys and mules. In former times it was here the grapes were gathered and the olives crushed into meal and olive-oil. And there in the small courtyard the millstones still lay, remnants of another age. The urns where Reo's parents had kept their wine and water remained intact, just where they had always been, and soon he was exploring the house of his childhood, simple but substantial.

Up the outside stair to the bedrooms and there he was, in the very room where first he saw the light of day; and there in the corner, still standing where it had stood eighty-five years earlier, the same iron bedstead in which he was born.

Life had come full circle and Reo Stakis was lost in thought, back in the peasant surroundings which had marked his early life and in which, for all the sophistication of the intervening years, he seemed comfortably at home.

This was Kato-Drys, a name meaning "lower pine" and once a busy community of five hundred souls, though now reduced to no more than two hundred, most of them elderly and many back home from their foreign adventures to spend their eventide years in the warmer climes of Cyprus. For it had long been the tradition of the young to leave home and go abroad, especially to Britain, Australia or the United States.

Reo's family name of Anastasis had been known in the village for generations, his father a hard-working man who, despite the olive-groves and plots of barley and wheat, was still a small farmer by most standards. There were the carob-trees and locust-beans you expect to find in Mediterranean countries.

On his mother's side, the family name was Girgallies and her father had been a local priest, at a level where the priesthood was considered compatible with marriage. Even today in the Greek Orthodox Church, further advancement requires the commitment to celibacy.

His mother, Katerina, was much younger than his father and quite clearly the object of her son's devotion. He can still wax eloquent about her qualities as a human being before launching into raptures about her God-given talent for the most exquisite embroidery and lace-work, which she conducted as a cottage industry. He will demonstrate how she would take paper and cut it, by free hand, into the most remarkable patterns for her lace-work. Yet, in the illiteracy of the time, part of the male chauvinism which expected their women to confine themselves to the home, this brilliant lady could neither read nor write.

Again in the tradition of the time—and one which persisted for another generation or more—her marriage was arranged through family, friends or neighbours seeking out the suitable partnerships and coming to an agreement which left little room for the fact that the couple might not even care for each other.

The theory was that love would grow, and the fortuitous outcome of such unions seems to have been that they lasted a good deal better than so-called love matches. Those old-fashioned virtues of self-discipline and determination appear to have played their part and divorce was hardly known. Dowries were involved in the marriage arrangement (a piece of land was often included) and Reo's father received some financial help from his father-in-law, the priest, who was not only spiritual leader of the community but a practising carpenter, like Jesus himself, making ploughs for the oxen.

Reo was the eldest of six children, born on 13th March, 1913, and followed by sisters Stella, Helen and Despina, brother Christopher and finally sister Erasmia. It was a pattern of four girls and two boys which he would repeat in his own later life, though in slightly different order.

His father had just one full-time employee but outside labour was brought in for the harvest, when they would gather in the olives and earn a shilling for a twelve-hour day. The locust-beans were brought in during July and August while the olives were collected through November and December. Local labour was hard to come by so the men came from central parts of the island. There was still the vineyard to plough and prune and much else to keep his father busy.

It was a hard life, the traditional struggle of the land, and young Reo was conscious of the need to work as a means of augmenting his pocket-money. From the age of twelve, he and another boy used to go out to the country and dig up a type of stone much in demand for house-building. Reo would load the stones on to a cart and they would haul their load back to the village to do a deal with the local builder. Paid per load, the two lads were each making five shillings a week, which seemed like a fortune in the 1920s.

Meanwhile his mother was busy organising the piece-working women who would follow her patterns of lace-making and bring it for inspection at the weekend, laying it out under that arched entrance to the yard which lies so silent today. Where there was once the happy chatter of industry within that family compound, there is little sign of life except for a couple of lemon trees which still flourish and produce the fruit which Reo Stakis regards as precious and essential to every healthy meal and drink.

The village church still stands today, elaborate in its interior decoration and filled with the portraits of saints who mean something to his tradition. Everywhere there is a priest or warden on hand to greet and to converse and without exception Sir Reo would know their family connections. Adjacent to the church stands the tiny school he attended from the end of the First World War in 1918. With such a small and aged population, Kato-Drys has little need for a school today. But in his time, between the wars, the division of the sexes was so strong that the boys were not even allowed to speak to the girls. So his school was for boys only.

Though Reo was keen on football, you had to come from a well-to-do family to afford a ball so, in a tradition also well-known to Scots children of the hungry days, they would bind together a bundle of rags and create their own makeshift ball. When they tired of that, they would turn to another game which was popular with Cypriot children; it was called lingri, not unlike basketball.

These recreations were a welcome break from the strict regime of the classroom, a severe approach to teaching of which Sir Reo thoroughly disapproved. It was based on fear and the memory of it was to stay with him for the rest of his life.

"They had teachers who had no patience whatsoever and they would beat us with sticks from the trees nearby," he could recall with a shudder. "I remember being told to go out and fetch those sticks. So we were nervous all the time and it is something I will never get over. As a result, I have been against that kind of thing ever since."

Children could leave school at twelve in those days but for the more promising there might be the chance of another two years of education at the American Academy in Larnaca. One of those boys was Reo Stakis. A contemporary from schooldays in Kato-Drys who followed the same route to Larnaca was Angelis Solomon, another who wandered the world before returning to his roots.

A thoughtful and kindly man in his mid-eighties, Angelis produced an illuminating picture of those days at the American missionary school. If Reo was not the cleverest boy in the class, he was certainly the most dedicated and hard-working, the smallest in stature but always the first to put up his hand with an answer.

No matter what he tackled, he seemed always determined to win.

And if that was an early insight into the kind of man he would become, Angelis remembered one incident in particular from their schooldays in Larnaca which in hindsight was quite prophetic. Evidently the teacher of Ancient Greek called the attention of the class one day and said: "Do you see that little boy there? One day he will be a great man."

The privilege of sending a gifted child to the Academy required parental sacrifice—twenty-two pounds a year to be precise—and the distance from home meant spending the term as a boarder, sharing a dormitory with boys like Angelis Solomon. Reo's father, who transported him to Larnaca by means of the family mule, could ill afford the expense, if the truth be known.

There were four sisters and another brother to be maintained and, for all his hard work in grinding other people's olives as well as his own, the plain fact was that ends were not meeting. In an attempt to keep his family afloat he had borrowed up to £400, a colossal figure at the time, and in the shadow of some bad years in farming, he was under pressure to pay back the money.

Crisis time had been reached in the Anastasis household. And however long he might have remained at school in Larnaca, young Reo now became the focus of attention as his father called him in for a heart-to-heart talk. The boy was still fourteen but, as the eldest child, he now had responsibilities which he well understood.

With the father so deeply in debt, his opening words were blunt and to the point: "Reo, you will have to go abroad and see what you can do."

3

TEARS AT THE QUAYSIDE

What Reo could do required no further explanation. There was already a tradition of Cypriots going abroad to sell the lace for which their womenfolk were famous. The neighbouring village of Lefkara, where he would eventually find his wife, was the most notable name in lace-making but there would be no woman in existence who could surpass the artistic genius of his own mother. So they did at least have a marketable product beyond compare and there was a relative who had been one of the pioneers of selling Cyprus lace in Britain.

For all that, however, we would think twice in this modern age about sending a boy of fourteen on a mission to foreign parts with a remit to carry a suitcase from door to door in the hope that he might persuade enough people to buy his wares. But needs must; and in retrospect he could recall that he faced the responsibility without fear or trepidation and not even with any sense of adventure. It was born out of necessity for his family's economic survival and he knew how much the folks back home would depend upon his efforts as a salesman.

We tend to forget, of course, that people in bygone times were far more mobile than we imagine and it testifies to their courage and ingenuity that, long before the days of simplified travel, they would undertake unthinkable journeys by the most basic means of transport. The achievement of the early explorers should tell us something about the history of human will and endurance.

In the Anastasis household, Katerina prepared a good selection of her finest work, tablecloths and mats, sideboard runners and embroidered bedclothes. She had packed a value of around £60 into that bundle as she turned her attention to the other suitcase which would contain the boy's personal belongings. Young Reo could only imagine his mother's thoughts as the hour of departure approached and he and his father mounted the donkey for their twenty-two mile journey to the port of Larnaca.

There could hardly have been a less auspicious start to an adventure which would change the whole course of their family life. With the other children gathered round, his mother waved him off, no doubt with a heaviness of heart for the boy who was still only fourteen years of age. As Kato-Drys disappeared in the distance, they trundled on down the valley towards the sea that day in 1928.

His grandfather had given some money to tide him over on his arrival in Britain and as they reached the quayside at Larnaca his father was preparing to hand over what little he could afford for the journey, the first stage of which would take the boy to the Greek port of Piraeus. Fumbling with his money, he handed over what came to a total of seven pounds.

Reo looked anxiously: "Will this be enough?"

He never forgot the sight of his father, standing there in his native costume, a pathetic figure who had given his all. "My father broke down and started crying. He gave me his open purse and said 'Look—I have nothing!' "

So they waved their goodbyes and as Cyprus receded in a heat-haze, Reo Stakis turned to take stock of his new surroundings. It was then that he ran into his first stroke of luck, which might have been an omen for the days ahead.

As the boat sailed round from the south side of Cyprus and up

17

towards the Greek port of Piraeus, Reo Stakis was delighted to spot the familiar face of a man from his own village of Kato-Drys. Quite unknown to him, George Frangos was not only heading for Piraeus but was set for exactly the same journey as himself. His destination was London and, what is more, his purpose was to sell Cyprus lace around the doors of Britain.

As a mature man, George had some experience of this business, having been on similar missions to the United States. As the two became instant friends, he took a fatherly interest in the boy and Reo, in turn, was able to help with his English, which was less than adequate. He at least was fresh from school. They slept on the open deck and Reo was anxious to keep an eye on his valuable cargo of lace.

From Piraeus they sailed on to Marseilles, which struck him as a beautiful city, though the feature which most appealed to him at first was the sight of the huge work-horses plying the streets. He could not believe the size of their hooves.

Young Reo was now on the final lap of his journey across Europe, with one thought in mind: How far could he succeed in wiping out his father's debts? He and George were now approaching Victoria Station in London for their very first view of this metropolis from which their native Cyprus was governed. They alighted from the train, walked along the platform to the main concourse and set down the cases to gain their bearings.

It was only a matter of seconds but suddenly there was consternation. Reo's case was gone! Which one? The one with the lace! Oh no! He hadn't even noticed the sneak thief who nipped in to relieve him of his entire stock and to vanish into thin air. In despair, he stood there crying and shouting for help. But if good luck was going to be a feature of young Stakis's life then it struck again in the vastness of Victoria Station, London. For a railway security man happened to spot the thief and gave chase. He caught him, recovered the case and was soon back, saying "Is this yours?"

Reo Stakis can still to this day shudder about the possible consequences of that experience. What on earth would he have done without his bag of lace? Such a twist of fate could have broken his spirit and sent him scampering back home with his mission already defeated and his confidence shattered. As it was, and reassured by the fortuitous presence of George Frangos, he harnessed his good fortune and prepared to meet the challenge of door-to-door trading in Britain.

This was, after all, the country which had ruled Cyprus since 1878, formally annexing it at the start of the First World War and turning it into a Crown Colony in 1925, just three years before his departure. As a citizen of the Empire, he already had British citizenship.

Once he had calmed down from the ordeal of Victoria Station, Reo joined George Frangos in a search for somewhere to stay. They found a room in Endell Street which would cost them ten shillings a week. It was a base from where they could begin the exploration of London, a city with the kind of urban vastness Reo had never imagined. In trying to assess the properties around Hyde Park, for example, he was frequently confused by what was a public building and what was a private residence where he might seek to sell his goods.

So those early days were more to do with discovery than selling and indeed it took a week or two before they managed to sell anything. By then they had decided to move from the heart of London to suburban areas like Wimbledon and out to Richmond. Reo was also facing a problem of his own youthfulness, finding that people were taking little notice of him, unwilling to treat the boy at all seriously.

He was also surprised to find how few people knew anything at all about Cyprus, even to the extent of where his native island could be found on the map. In short, he was having a tough time. But he and George soldiered on together, Reo taking one side of the street and George the other. When people refused to see him, George would amuse Reo from across the street by shouting: "It's all right, I'll be back!"

Plodding on with his own side of the street, Reo learned a lesson from a kind old lady who showed some compassion, asked him to open his case and was astonished by the quality of what he had to sell. "But you shouldn't call it lace," she advised. "This is beautiful embroidery. In this country when you speak of lace people are more inclined to think of the things you tie your shoes with."

London was proving difficult so the two Cypriots decided to head out of town, with Liverpool as the first destination. The Merseyside welcome was much warmer though the ratio of sales to the amount of door-knocking was still too low. With the number of refusals, they had to keep going to make any kind of living and Reo would reflect on the experience, valuable though it was, and wonder how he had summoned up the patience to cope with it.

In those days so many of the houses seemed to have maids who answered the door. They would disappear inside and come back with the standard reply from the lady of the house: "No thank you, not today." There was some consolation in the fact that he was staying in digs with a sympathetic landlady, Mrs Nicolson, a Greek woman who had married a British soldier in the First World War.

While it could be a disheartening job, not always eliciting politeness, Reo felt that he was doing better than George. Together they moved on to their next city, which was Newcastle, and that was where they decided to part company and go their separate ways. Among his many discoveries, the young lad realised his name was difficult for the customers and that was when he decided to shorten Argiros Anastasis to the simpler Reo Stakis. The rest of the family back home took their cue from the young wanderer and they all became known as Stakis.

By then he was showing an ability to learn from experience.

Counteracting his boyish appearance, he had now taken to wearing striped trousers and a bowler hat, rather a fancy outfit for a lad still only sixteen, but from then onwards there was no doubt that business began to improve.

4

A LETTER TO THE QUEEN

Postal communication in those days was much quicker and more reliable than we might expect and Reo was constantly in touch with the folks back home. Fresh supplies of his mother's lace kept catching up with him at pre-arranged postal points and, as discerning customers began to appreciate the sheer quality of his merchandise, the lad was quick to develop selling methods which were better than knocking on doors at random, in what the modern world describes as "cold-calling."

From now on he would do business by recommendation, with a customer in Newcastle passing him on to an aunt in Glasgow, so that he arrived on the next doorstep with a ready-made introduction, thus eliminating so many wasteful calls. The businessman within the young Cypriot was developing quickly.

Having arrived in 1928, he paid his first visit back home two years later, by now prospering sufficiently that he was able to bring a particular joy to the family. As a result of Reo's adventures in Britain, the main purpose of his mission was now being achieved: his father's debts were being successfully cleared off. There were smiles all round.

But now that he was geared to this kind of activity, there was more to be done for the family. Next on the agenda would be schooling for the rest of the family. The sisters would be sent to higher education in Limassol while brother Christopher was off to Nicosia. Proudly achieving his first objective, Reo was being treated like the young man returning from abroad with his fortune already made. If it wasn't quite like that, he was certainly doing very well as a salesman, gaining all-round favour with that cheery smile emanating from Mediterranean good looks. There was also much curiosity and admiration for one so young whose basic story so far was one of enterprise and courage.

Back in Britain, where he had originally travelled by train, he was moving more freely by motorbike and sidecar, having paid £39 for an AJS model which was much in fashion at the time and took him more directly to his clients, with the greater facility for carrying his stock. By 1933 he was able to afford a car, buying himself a Morris Cowley which added comfort and prestige to his operation.

From Newcastle in the north-east of England the natural progression was across the border at Berwick-upon-Tweed and northwards to Edinburgh. The Scottish capital made an immediate and deep impression on the young Greek Cypriot, subconsciously perhaps commending itself with the characteristics which had made it known as the Athens of the North. Edinburgh was uniquely picturesque, dividing its Old Town from the fashionable New Town with the main thoroughfare of Princes Street, which had prestigious shops along one side and an open vista to the historic Edinburgh Castle on the other.

Already on his travels throughout Britain he was gathering tales to tell. In Manchester, for example, he used to stay in the digs once occupied by Charlie Chaplin, when he was touring the music halls with the Fred Karno show before heading off to fame and fortune in America.

From the days of his motorbike, Reo had made it his business to visit castles and mansion houses, at that time the more likely customers for high-quality lace. Wherever he went the cheery face attracted attention and that led to many a connection, even in aristocratic circles, which endured throughout the years. The arrival in Edinburgh, with its architectural splendours, put another idea in his head.

Enterprising or audacious, whichever you choose, he sat down one evening in his lodgings at 13 Union Street and wrote a personal letter to Queen Mary no less, the wife of King George V, and delivered it to the Palace of Holyroodhouse at the foot of the famous Royal Mile, their main residence when visiting Scotland.

Would Her Majesty be interested in buying his Cyprus lace? The shrewd calculation was that a young man of the Empire showing this kind of courage was not going to be lightly turned away. Nor was he. In due course there was an invitation to bring his samples to the palace so off he went down the Royal Mile, in a state of some excitement, to deliver his parcel to the lady-in-waiting.

Queen Mary did indeed like his mother's fancywork and when he returned for the verdict the royal attendant was waiting with a cheque for thirteen pounds. It was signed "Mary." Reo made his courteous retreat, examined the precious document and vowed he would never cash that royal cheque. He never did and it became a prized exhibit for years to come. One of the miseries of his later life was that he somehow mislaid the proof of that royal transaction.

But he was to renew the royal connection in years to come when he began to display at the Ideal Homes Exhibition at Olympia. The whole Royal Family came to visit his stand, led by Queen Elizabeth and Prince Philip. He still chuckles about the fact that, when Her Majesty led the entourage to its next destination, her husband stayed behind for a chat with Reo, muttering something about "Oh to hell with them!"

They were destined to meet again on several occasions, of course, not least when the sword would touch his shoulder; but all that was a long way in the future. Back in the 1930s, the foundations of his life in Britain were still being laid. From his initial love affair with Edinburgh, he headed west to Glasgow, little knowing what part that city would play in his career, before heading north to Aberdeen, Inverness and Thurso, extending his vast knowledge of Great Britain all the way from Land's End to John o' Groats.

By his next visit home to Cyprus, in 1936, he was driving the Singer car which was involved in that near-tragedy in the Troodos Mountains but which symbolised the prosperity attending his foreign adventure. It was a stunning performance by any standard. Still only twenty-three, he had completely cleared his father's worrying debts and afforded the best possible education for his five siblings, enabling them to reach beyond their peasant background in Kato-Drys to the academies of Larnaca and Limassol.

At one stage in the mid-1930s Reo even brought his father to Scotland to help him sell his mother's lace. It was a memorable experience for the old man but he was like a fish out of his Mediterranean waters, with very little English and finding it difficult to adjust to another country. His son would take him into a restaurant in Glasgow and observe his means of ordering a dish.

Unsure of himself, he would look around the tables to see what other people were eating. Then he would point to one which took his fancy and call out "I'll have that!" He was soon back home, however, and always looking forward to welcoming Reo, who made his periodic visits right up to the outbreak of the Second World War in 1939.

His father died in the first year of that war, at least with an easy mind over those debts which he had accumulated only from a desire to do the best by his family. Reo may not yet have been making a fortune but, on those visits home, he was taking back sums approaching a thousand pounds—and that seemed not far short of a fortune in those more impoverished times.

5

WITH MATRIMONY IN MIND

The affairs of the heart may be universal but the ritual of finding a wife still varies dramatically between east and west, even at the end of the twentieth century. Old habits die hard in Cyprus, which hovers between east and west, and in Reo Stakis's young day, and indeed for at least a generation later, it would fall to people like him as the eldest son to find suitable husbands for his sisters.

But first of all, he had to find a wife for himself. By 1939 he had decided the moment had arrived and went off to set the process in motion, returning to his native island with one purpose in mind. In fact, the mood would be appropriate because he was also due to attend a local wedding in Kato-Drys. Of prime importance in the Greek culture was to choose someone of good family which meant that, in those small villages, they had developed a reliable network of intelligence about who was good and who was not!

If he was keeping the matter close to his chest, the truth was that Reo had already earmarked the family of good name and had an instinct for the particular young lady who might one day be his bride. By chance, he knew her brother Peter but had yet to set eyes on Anna Petropoulos. Curiously, just as it would be his duty to find husbands for his four sisters, they in turn played a vital part, unwittingly, in finding a wife for brother Reo.

Home from their boarding school in Limassol, they kept talking about Anna, with whom they shared a dormitory. In the mysterious process of natural selection, the fates seemed to be planting a name in his subconscious.

Anna Petropoulos came from that neighbouring village of Lefkara, true home of lace-making in which her father had established a very substantial business. Originally he had taken his wife to live in Paris, where he was selling to the fashionable shops, but she pined for Cyprus and her widowed mother, so she returned to conduct the supply of lace from Lefkara, despatching six boxes every week, while her husband continued to spend the rest of his business life in the French capital, coming home periodically to see the family.

Whatever the hazards of separation, the situation made for a prosperous living, as reflected not only in an impressive home in the centre of Lefkara but a country house as well, distinguished by its windmill. Nicolas Petropoulos saw to it that his children wanted for nothing. While Anna (or Annitsa, as we shall come to know her) was sent to boarding school in Limassol, brother Peter had finished at the Greek College in Nicosia and was spending a year with his father in Paris, studying at the French Academie and preparing for entry to Oxford University, where he would read law.

At the boarding school in Limassol, Annitsa found herself forging friendships with the two sisters from Kato-Drys, Despina and Helen Anastasis. On occasions when the headmistress addressed the pupils, it became something of a habit for her to raise the example of this wonderful man, Reo, from whose beneficence his sisters were privileged to be at this school. It was one of those repetitive homilies which in time could induce a yawn, as paragons of virtue tend to do.

While sweet sixteen and still at school, Annitsa was due to be a bridesmaid at a wedding in neighbouring Kato-Drys—the same wedding for which the wonderful Reo was heading home from

Britain. A delay in the journey meant that he missed the wedding ceremony and Annitsa was preparing to leave for home when the bold adventurer rolled up in his fine motor car, in time to catch the tail-end of the reception.

There were no fancy hotels for weddings in those pre-war days, just a feast and dancing in the bride's home, for however many the place could hold. When Reo Stakis arrived and found that Annitsa and some friends were just leaving, he insisted they stay on.

He asked her to dance and this became the pattern for the remainder of the evening. Such was the family concern of those days that her parents came searching from Lefkara to see why she had not come home.

The first step had been taken towards the union of Reo Stakis and Annitsa Petropoulos, though their opportunities to become thoroughly acquainted would remain limited. Reo arrived at her home in Lefkara to ask if she would be bridesmaid at a family wedding but, while she was seeing more of him, she was not aware of any burning romantic notions a-stirring in her soul.

Her thoughts were focused on further education and in any case she felt she was too young to be thinking more seriously about men. But the weight of tradition was not in her favour. Father took her aside and said pointedly: "That's a good boy!" The inference was that she should not miss the chance. He added: "A man who loves his family like that will love his wife as well."

There was much homespun philosophy and wisdom in the Greek tradition. They lived by certain tenets which may now have gone out of fashion and are sometimes the butt of ridicule but which have a habit of coming back to haunt us when the so-called sophistications of modern life collapse.

Having found the good family name, and the suitable girl within that family, Reo Stakis knew that very soon he would be able to love her. His purpose now set, he needed to pursue it with vigour and there was no doubting his determination as he set out that day from Kato-Drys on the short journey to Lefkara. Having turned up at the Petropoulos residence, he was there not only to negotiate an official request to Nicolas, the father, but to hear it from the lips of Annitsa, the daughter, that she would wish to marry him.

Though there had now been more time to consult her feelings, she still felt she was too young and that there were other possibilities in life. Within the fold of strict family tradition, it was not an easy decision but she did go off to consider it from all angles and came back with the answer her suitor wanted to hear.

All was now set for an early marriage. He was twenty-six, she was just turning seventeen. Reo Stakis, accompanied by Annitsa's brother Peter, who was by now studying law at Oxford, set out for Britain to tidy up some matters before returning to Cyprus for the wedding. The arrangement was that they would be back in forty days.

Within those forty days, however, the Second World War broke out—and the bride-to-be did not see her man again for six years! At the distance of sixty years, it is hard to appreciate the impossibility of foreign travel during the war, except on military service, and even the difficulty of receiving letters from abroad. There were periods when Annitsa had to content herself with the occasional telegram from Reo and Peter saying simply "We are well."

As with any other girl in that society, there was the added restriction of being an engaged young lady. In such a tradition of strict parental control, etiquette dictated that, throughout the wartime separation, she could be seen talking to her own cousins and to members of Reo's family but certainly not to any grown male outwith that circle. There was the dread that such an indiscretion might be misinterpreted and reported back to Reo.

Such frustrations could have produced two quite different reactions. As it happened, Annitsa Petropoulos found that absence did indeed make the heart grow fonder.

There had now been more than enough time to assess her feelings and by the time her Reo came home in 1945, all the doubts of the immature girl had disappeared, and her purpose was now clear and strong. With a positive love, she was ready to be his wife.

By now, she was grieving for a beloved mother who had died in 1943, at the age of forty-three, and the only consolation was that she had lived to know the man who would look after her daughter for the rest of their lives.

Meanwhile, Reo Stakis had spent those war years in Britain, where he volunteered for the Royal Air Force in Glasgow but was rejected on the grounds of a heart condition. As a British citizen, however, he served in the Home Guard, better known to later generations under its television title of "Dad's Army."

While Reo found himself in Britain for the duration, most of his kinsfolk who had been selling lace in this country managed to make it back home to Cyprus in haste, leaving their stocks of lace behind. He bought up those stocks at favourable prices and continued his business as before. After all, life had to go on and his supplies were now so large that they would last until the late 1940s, with no need for further consignments from home.

Even before the outbreak of war, his success in the business of selling lace had reached proportions which were substantial by the standards of the United Kingdom and therefore quite staggering in terms of the economy in Cyprus. It helped to explain the miracles he had already been able to perform for the folks back home and give some clue as to what he might be able to afford in the years immediately ahead.

Although they would befriend one another, those lace-sellers from Cyprus were naturally in competition and kept fairly much to themselves in those years between the wars. That applied even to his own uncle, Achille Papadopoulo, who he would meet in places like Aberdeen and Inverness. But Achille at least took a fatherly interest in the young man and was alarmed when he bought a motorbike. "You'll kill yourself!" he warned.

But when Reo moved on to motor cars his uncle had second thoughts and felt there might be something in this progress business after all. He even asked if Reo would teach him to drive. But in time he went off home to Cyprus, just as George Frangos, the man Reo had met on the journey to Britain, went off back to America, where he had been before. Neither of these older men had done so well in the selling of lace as young Reo, whose secret had lain in that change-over from random calling to a more methodical way of working.

On Royal Deeside, for example, he arranged with the manager of the Fife Arms Hotel in Braemar to stage an exhibition of his wares. It was a resounding success, which he extended to other hotels, always working towards better methods of selling.

With the triumph of acquiring Queen Mary as a customer, Reo had little fear of those mighty mansions as he strode up the driveway of an impressive pile called Glentyan at Kilbarchan, near Glasgow, complete with its profusion of rhododendrons.

As he turned out his wares, the lady of the house was deeply impressed by the quality of his mother's lace and said she would like embroidered runners for this very large table. In another room there was a dresser which could be doing with a lace covering.

Young Reo had seldom seen a house like this, nor had he had an order so big. Back at his digs, he sat down with much excitement to write a letter to his mother, with this very special order which would keep her busy for some time. When the lace eventually arrived in Scotland, he headed out to Kilbarchan, only to be met with a reception rather different from what he expected.

He was now confronted by the man of the house, who was taking a very different view from that of his wife. The young bagman was virtually being told to beat it, even when he pleaded that he was only delivering the lace which had been ordered. The wife appeared nervously in the background but the husband had the last word and Reo Stakis walked away with a heavy heart, knowing that his mother had wasted a great deal of time and effort.

Ah well. You couldn't win them all, they said. But there was a sequel to that story which would lie a whole generation ahead.

Travelling around the country, Reo Stakis had developed another interest in life. In his nomadic existence, he was eating in a great variety of restaurants and coming to the conclusion that there was much room for improvement in Britain's catering industry. Conversely, he was quick to spot the establishments which did meet with his approval and one of those was Farley's on Edinburgh's Leith Walk.

The boss himself was not at all responsive when Reo tried to make his acquaintance, resisting the Stakis charm perhaps because he suspected a potential rival. Little did he know! Reo nevertheless could sense the success of Farley's place and was mentally noting the features which seemed to contribute to that success. A notion was stirring somewhere at the back of his mind. The seeds of a future restaurateur were already being sown.

But there were other more immediate matters to be attended to back home in Cyprus, like finding husbands for his sisters—and providing dowries for their marriages. It was all part of the tradition.

In fact, by the time war broke out he had already settled two of the four successfully in marriage. Fate had taken a hand one day when, walking down Tottenham Court Road in London he heard his name called out. "Reo Stakis!" said the man from a distance. He turned round. "Alex Costa! What are you doing here?"

Alex had been a fellow-pupil at the Academy back home, staying on after Reo's time to complete his education and become a teacher. Now, however, he had entered the hotel business and was working as a commis-waiter in London. There was a Lyon's Corner House nearby so they found a table to themselves and began catching up with old times. It was the chance renewal of a friendship which would have its own repercussions and confirm the mysterious workings of a fate which seems to shape our destiny.

Reo and Alex began to see more and more of each other until the former said to his friend one day: "How would you like to join me in selling lace?" Alex jumped at the chance and was soon making a decent living for himself. Reo was assessing just how good a man he had become; good enough in fact to be a husband for one of the Stakis sisters. He raised the name of Stella and suggested he might want to go back home, decide if she could be the right woman for him and then ask his father to make contact with the Stakis family.

It was all within the ritual—and the instincts were working well. Alex Costa did indeed follow the suggested path and ended up by marrying Stella. Reo brought them to Scotland and, just as Alex had joined him in selling lace, he would later become a key figure in Reo's subsequent career, with a family home in the Pollokshields district of Glasgow. On the personal level, Alex would also become his very best friend, a fine-looking man with teeth like pearls.

Reo reflected on his good fortune in meeting Alex Costa in London that day, having already lined up for Stella another suitor who turned out to be a rogue. He too came from a nearby village in Cyprus and Reo had at first thought he was of good family and proper substance. He later concluded, however, that the man's thoughts had been on the dowry because he suddenly disappeared to the United States.

But this was just the start of the matchmaking. In Scotland, he caught up with another man from the village back home, born Charalambous Nikolaou but anglicising it to Harry Nicholas. In 1936 he had followed the path to London, where his older brother was a head waiter at Claridges.

Harry was of good family and Reo Stakis was soon marking him out as a potential husband for sister Despina. In this case,

Harry had the advantage of knowing the girl and the path of true matchmaking ran smoothly. They were soon married and living in Scotland, becoming well-known in time as mine host and hostess of the Glynhill Hotel at Renfrew, which they opened in 1970.

Then came sister Helen, a beautiful and intelligent girl whose future husband was found through a recommendation from Alex Costa. He said he knew a man he considered suitable for the role and undertook to make the initial approach. That, too, resulted in marriage and Helen and Chris Simeonides came to live in Edinburgh, where their son would eventually become the Greek Consul.

That left Erasmia as the last challenge to his talent for finding husbands. A chap called Socrates Christodoulides worked for Reo in Glasgow before going to London, starting his own surveyor's business and becoming a lecturer at King's College. Reo's mission of matrimony was complete.

6

SIR LAURENCE FOR SUPPER

Those machinations of matrimony had straddled the Second World War but now that that conflict was over, Reo Stakis was back in Cyprus for his own auspicious event, which was arranged to take place in the Greek Orthodox Church in Annitsa's home village of Lefkara on Sunday, 12th May 1946.

It is hard to grasp that, in those colonial days, the British officials rarely spoke to local people, except when they had to. In Britain, however, there was nothing to stop Reo making friends with whoever he liked. He happened to form a friendship with a family called Armitage, one of whom was the Governor of Cyprus, and when he went back home at the end of the war, that contact gave him an entrée to the Governor's Palace in Nicosia.

In the context of the time, this was considered a remarkable event, a real breakthrough, in that nobody from the peasant villages had ever been to the palace. That handsome edifice would in time become the Presidential Palace, residence of the head of state, where Reo Stakis came to be a regular and welcome visitor.

Even so soon after the war, however, Reo Stakis had established such good credentials that a prominent colonial was a best-man at that spring wedding of 1946. And what a jolly affair it turned out to be, with that massive guest-list splitting in two, for receptions at their respective villages of Lefkara and Kato-Drys, a labyrinth of family connection where everyone was more than welcome.

It was certainly a day to remember in those peasant villages by the lower slopes of Cyprus and none was more proud that Reo's mother, Katerina, by now a widow but looking fondly on the son who had saved their sanity by going off to Britain while still a slip of a boy, making such a success of his life that he had not only paid off her husband's debts but educated the rest of her family as well.

Reo in turn idolised his mother, with all her sterling qualities, and was so keen to make up for time lost during the war that he was in no hurry to return to his well-established life in Britain. So he and Annitsa spent the first eight months of their married life in Cyprus before deciding it was time to set out for their new home, in the city of Glasgow, which had by now become the favoured centre of Reo's business.

In preparation for bringing his young bride to Scotland in 1946, he had already bought a house. And as a sign of how well he had prospered, that house was the spacious residence at 54 Aytoun Road, Pollokshields, which would remain the family home for the next forty years. The house, which was still in his possession at the end of the century, cost him £2000, compared with a more recent valuation of £300,000. What's more, he was able to put down the total price. Not a mortgage in sight!

Until the final months of the Second World War, Reo was still fully engaged in the selling of lace, while casting an eye on the catering industry which was now taking his fancy. He had always been interested in food and that restaurant in Leith had given him ideas. Now, with the approach of peacetime, his hunches were telling him that, if he intended to make the change, this was the time to do it.

Among the lace-selling Cypriots he had met on his travels around Britain was Charles Pattichis, yet another from his own village of Kato-Drys, which had proved a prolific source of salesmen for all the size of its population. He had also befriended Michael Epifaniou, another fellow-countryman, and it was to Charles and Michael that Reo Stakis put the proposition: How about the three of us going into business as caterers?

None of them knew anything about it but all were willing to give it a try. "All I could do at that time was boil water," is how Reo remembers the early venture. The three men invested £500 each, found themselves modest premises in Hope Street, Glasgow, and looked around for a suitable name. With the reigning mood of celebration at the end of the war, the word on everyone's lips was "Victory." So the astute Stakis decided that that would be the name of their little restaurant, which had seating capacity for forty people.

In the bleak austerity of that post-war period, the three musketeers were learning to bring a welcome touch of cuisine from their Greek background, which was a novelty at the time. Reo steeped himself in the new role, alternating his energies between working in the kitchen and serving in the restaurant.

But his enthusiasm was not shared by Charles and Michael and before the year was out they had withdrawn their investment in the Victory—and Reo was on his own as a caterer for the very first time. Little could he have guessed where that humble beginning was going to lead him.

Already he was working out a strategy of business and planning to expand, identifying his niche which would not yet aspire to the top end of the market. That belonged to the famous Malmaison Restaurant, which was part of the Glasgow Central Hotel but with its own separate entrance on Hope Street, just a short distance from the Victory. The Malmaison was without doubt the city's best.

But there were opportunities in the middle range and that would be his next aim. From that modest beginning at the Victory, he opened on the other side of Hope Street, at its junction with

Sauchiehall Street, with a restaurant he would call the Acropole. Reo Stakis was learning quickly, gaining a fine reputation for quality food which was drawing a high calibre of clientèle.

Justifiably claiming that he had introduced Greek food to Glasgow, he splashed out on a high-profile opening of his new premises, inviting the Lord Provost of the city, Sir Patrick Dollan, to perform the ceremony. The natural charm which had served him well in selling lace was transferring very easily to his new business and the personal approach to Sir Patrick not only brought a positive response but sparked off a lasting friendship between them.

The Scots, who knew little of foreign food at the time and were suspicious of most of it, were finding that Greek cuisine was very much to their taste. It was simple, wholesome and everything was edible—and the Acropole had a chef who knew how to serve it at its best.

As a result of this reputation, you would find the most unexpected people dining there. Appearing at Glasgow theatres like the Alhambra, Sir Laurence Olivier would come to the Acropole for supper after the show. Reo Stakis struck up a friendship with Sir Laurence and his wife of the time, Vivien Leigh, who was still fresh in the public mind from her Oscar-winning role of Scarlett O'Hara in *Gone With The Wind*. Charles Laughton became another friend from those theatre visits to Glasgow.

Now that he had gained a taste for the catering industry, Reo was in a hurry to expand. Soon he was caught up in a burst of activity which would initiate him into the hurly-burly of business, show him the shadier side of capitalism and teach him a few lessons about how to handle negotiations.

As we have seen, Stakis fell very much into that category of door-to-door salesman who, in an age gone by, came to know his customers extremely well. In many a rural district the annual visit of such people became an event to be anticipated with pleasure. The Onion Johnnies from France were an example of a tradition where generations of sellers would be known to succeeding generations of customers, with much inquiry about the young families and the old folks back home.

Reo Stakis had something more enduring than onions to offer and those friendships never failed to delight him, producing patterns of acquaintance which could be as intricate and lasting as the Cypriot lace he was offering for sale.

Through his regular visits to the community of Busby, on the south side of Glasgow, he came to know the Bannantyne family, the father of the house being chairman of the Scottish Temperance Life Association, the big financial house which had its headquarters in St Vincent Street, Glasgow.

Now that he had forsaken the delicacy of lace for that of cuisine, Reo mentioned to Mr Bannantyne that if ever that basement belonging to his company became available, he would be interested in turning it into a restaurant. It was while he was back in Cyprus for his wedding that a telegram arrived from Glasgow. Mr Bannantyne was letting him know that the basement had indeed become available and asking if he was still interested.

Reo was impressed that his old customer had not only remembered about it but was keeping his word and giving him first refusal. Even though his mind was on matters more personal and romantic, time had to be found for the reply to that telegram: "Yes, very interested." And that was how Glasgow came to have its Ivy Restaurant in St Vincent Street.

7

IN A TIZZY WITH IZZY

The Ivy Restaurant became known as a popular coffee-house, attracting many a Glasgow businessman between 10 and 11am. Reo Stakis was giving it his full professional attention, welcoming customers and forging friendships with people like Isidore A. Walton, the well-known tycoon who had founded Scottish Metropolitan, the big property company.

In the flush of enthusiasm for his expanding business, Stakis was telling Walton about his plans, the most exciting of which at that moment concerned a projected restaurant in Sauchiehall Street which would aim at the upper end of the market under the name of L'Apéritif. This would more than rival the famous Ferrari's Restaurant in the same street, an establishment he much admired.

The premises were in the hands of a local auctioneer with whom Stakis had reached agreement for their purchase and it needed only the formality of signing the documents. A few days later, the story goes, Walton turned up for his morning coffee at the Ivy and exchanged the usual cordial greeting with his friend Reo.

In the course of their casual conversation Izzy, as he was commonly known, said: "Oh by the way, Reo, those premises in Sauchiehall Street you were talking about. I have just bought them!"

"You've what?" said a flabbergasted Stakis. "I thought you were a friend."

There was just a shrug. Business was business and Izzy had got there first with the signature that mattered. But he was in the property market and of course Reo would have the first chance to secure his proposed new site at a rental of £4000 a year. But it was worth only £1000. Walton had him over a barrel.

Alternatively, he could make an offer to buy it and Izzy was trying him out with a price of £95,000. Stakis knew he was talking ridiculous money and said he would offer £28,000 but would agree to the price set by an independent valuer. Walton agreed to take that chance too—and had to settle for just £1000 above the offer price. Stakis had at least secured the future of his new restaurant for £29,000, perhaps not much more than it would have cost if Walton had not interfered.

By now, of course, he had imparted more of his business confidences to Mr Walton, unaware that such naivety was something he would have to control. Another venture he had mentioned was the plan to open a restaurant called The Princes in Renfield Street, again with a verbal agreement of first option to buy.

Walton had also tucked away that piece of intelligence and was back at the Ivy in an incredibly short time with another of his bombshells: "Ah Reo, that place you were talking about. I've just bought that one too! But you can have it at a rental of £5000."

Stakis was apoplectic, passing judgement on "a dreadful man," a view he retained throughout his life, while contrasting him with his son and successor, David Walton, for whom he gained respect. Stakis was being dealt some salutary lessons which he would not forget, not only about security but on how deals have to be finalised without delay.

His instinct told him, however, that there might be some doubt about this latest Walton shock. Was it really as cut-and-dried as the man was making out? He immediately contacted his lawyer, Hugh

T. McCalman, and asked him to go to Nottingham to see the owners of the property and to find out how far this deal had really gone.

McCalman was on the Nottingham doorstep in no time, discovering that Isidore Walton had certainly made an offer for the whole block and the deal was due to be signed on the following week. He was smartly on the phone to Stakis. What had Walton offered? Around £200,000? Add £50,000 to that, Stakis instructed. McCalman signed the deal before he left Nottingham.

There was just one problem: Where was Stakis to get the money? At that moment, if the truth were known, he didn't have a penny to his name. But all business was a matter of buying and selling, borrowing and paying back, which explained so many of the mysteries which forever baffle the man-in-the-street, who cannot understand how so-and-so can lay hands on that kind of finance.

At that precise moment, he simply didn't have the money. And that is where confidence comes into play. When he set out for Edinburgh that day, Reo Stakis knew exactly where he was going. Once again, the connections from the lace-selling years were turning up trumps. Or so he hoped!

In those early days he had sold his mother's work to an Edinburgh family of some substance, the head of the household being Sir John, later Lord, Erskine, managing director of the old Commercial Bank before amalgamations brought it under the wing of the Royal Bank of Scotland. (Lord Erskine was later Governor of Northern Ireland from 1964 till 1968).

Stakis was armed with full details of his proposed transaction, realising that bankers deal in hard facts and not in the fantasies of fledgling businessmen who don't have a penny in their pockets. Then again, there is that matter of having an instinct for people.

Sir John listened to his former doorstep salesman, who was just getting into his stride. He listened a little longer and then said: "Yes, well, I'll get you the cheque. Now can we go and have some lunch?"

Reo Stakis paused and didn't believe his ears. Surely this could not be the speed and nonchalance with which a top banker could reach a decision and move on to the more mundane matter of his stomach. Signing over £250,000 just like that?

Still not convinced, he said: "But Sir John, did you hear what I was saying?"

Of course he heard. And they did move on to a lunch where the young customer's digestion took time to settle. Back in Glasgow on the Monday morning, Reo waited for the bouncy Mr Walton to appear as usual for his coffee. He duly turned up, wanting an answer to his proposition about renting the property. After all, there would be other interested parties.

"Oh yes," said Stakis. No, he wouldn't be interested in renting it. "As a matter of fact," he said, "I have just bought that whole block you were supposed to have bought!"

"You've what?"

"You heard," said Stakis. Yes, he heard but he still didn't believe it. "Where did you get that kind of money?" he demanded, somewhat insolently.

"That," said Reo Stakis with immense satisfaction, "is none of your business."

On this occasion he had learned to funnel his anger in a fruitful direction. There was, after all, something in that business maxim which advised: "Don't get mad, get even."

So now he had his Princes Restaurant as well as L'Apéritif, which was not far from Mr Ferrari's popular establishment; in fact the latter could be seen passing his rival's door every day at lunchtime, checking on how the fifty-seater was doing. From the first day it was doing very well and from a starting-point of commercial espionage, Stakis and Ferrari became good friends.

People were still finding it hard to resist the friendly face of the man from Cyprus, as witness the story told by the late George Rex Stewart, who was just starting on the road to prominence with his advertising and public relations business. His office at that time was situated directly above the Princes Restaurant in Renfield Street, to which Reo Stakis was giving his undivided attention.

It was at the Princes that Reo had introduced one of his most successful innovations, the spit-chicken business. Offering a carry-out service, he could turn thirty-six chickens at a time and the public were queueing up to buy them. It was one of those novelties which catch the public imagination and it was not unusual to be selling 1500 of his Aberdeenshire birds on a Saturday alone.

The downside of this novelty was that the heating arrangement was inclined to produce unintended fires in the kitchen and on more than one occasion the conflagration was toasting the feet of Rex Stewart in the room above. Rex had never met the little Cypriot but decided it was time to go down and have it out with him.

Duly fired with anger, he started out—but later confessed that once he confronted the cheery little chap he simply couldn't be cross with him. Apologies and assurances were duly accepted and the two men became close friends forever after.

The Princes was actually a complex of restaurants spread over four floors. From Renfield Street you could enter a cocktail bar in the basement, a restaurant on the ground floor and the Blue Room, which served continental food and was the popular haunt of showbusiness people like Andy Stewart and journalists who included popular author Jack House. From a separate entrance in Bath Street you found your way to the brand new Copacabana, for the opening of which Mr Stakis engaged the appropriate figure of Edmundo Ros, leader of the best-known Latin American band in the country.

As a further sequel to that encounter with Izzy Walton, which brought him the Princes Restaurant as part of the whole block, he negotiated deals by which other tenants, such as Hutton's shoe shop, bought their respective premises and Stakis was left with his Princes Restaurant for nothing. Sir John Erskine's faith in the man from the Mediterranean had not been misplaced. And the fact that these other tenants had not been overcharged for their purchase was borne out when Hutton's soon resold the shoe shop for twice the money. Reo liked to think that, in any deal, there was something in it for everyone. That particular block was later to become British Home Stores.

8

GLAMOROUS GIRLS

By the time these business deals were accelerating, Reo and Annitsa were well established in their substantial villa in leafy Pollokshields. For all her attachment to their homeland, Annitsa was quite happy to be leaving for an entirely different environment, by now wholly committed to the man she knew would be her partner for life.

Not unexpectedly, as a stranger in a strange land she was desperately lonely at first and found the early years something of a trial. But she soon realised that Reo had gathered around him a wonderful circle of friends and the womenfolk of those families were seeing to it that the young lady from Cyprus did not want for company and that there was a social round of coffee mornings and outings available to her if she so wished. After all, being the wife of a tycoon tied up in his business could have its problems.

But soon there was a family, with so much happening at Aytoun Road that Annitsa didn't have to think about how to occupy her time. In August 1947, the year after their marriage, she gave birth to Katerina, who was given the paternal grandmother's name, to be shortened to Rena. Three more girls were to follow in the next four years: Niki Rhoda, who would be Niki, Evridiki, who became Ridi, and Anastassia, who was to be known as Stassia.

With the male offspring proving elusive, there was a gap of more than four years before the first boy was born in April 1956.

He would be called Andros, to be followed three years later by another boy, Evros.

From the 1950s, therefore, they were growing up as a bustling, energetic family, the girls living up to that tradition of dark, Mediterranean good looks. All six began their education at a private school in Pollokshields called St Ronan's, run by a formidable educationist, Mrs Kemmet, whose husband and sons were all prominent journalists with Lord Beaverbrook's Express Newspapers in Glasgow, London and Paris.

Rena was first to arrive at St Ronan's but remembers it mainly in Dickensian terms, with a particular memory of her first teacher, a forbidding lady of the Victorian spinster variety who was not averse to slapping you across the face. Andros has no better memories of a strict regime. Having accidentally pulled a button from a boy's jacket during a game, he was hauled in and belted, and remained bewildered by the punishment.

At home, he looked up to the four older sisters, who influenced him in their different ways. He had a special relationship with Ridi, who he remembers as "the calm one, like an angel to me, who spoke soft words and showed me kindness and knew exactly how to handle me." Niki was sporty, bright and dynamic, the one he felt he came to resemble the most. Stassia was a battler, feeling she had to prove things on the way to becoming an actress, as she did.

The children felt in retrospect that they had been quite a handful and that their mother, in her diligence, had been overworked. Reo and Annitsa were traditionalists and, from the strength of his deep love for his parents, Andros thought he could afford to be critical and say that one of their mistakes was on focusing on himself and "the reserve son, Evros" as the two who would follow the tradition.

He said: "There was a lot of talent in the family but, with the traditional background, the girls had to suffer and they became rebellious. For us all it was difficult being brought up in the Greek manner but in another country. It was much like being a Muslim. Personally I suffered from an identity problem and Glasgow Academy did nothing for my confidence. Academically, it was a good school but I found it to be slightly bigoted."

Andros was a bright academic, a member of the Oxbridge class, a chess enthusiast and one of the top tennis players in the school, as well as a member of the first XV at rugby. For all that, he was conscious of the fact that they did not make him a prefect. He looked towards one particular teacher, Chick Varley, and felt he had faith in him. But it took only one remark from a favourite master to deflate him: "Of course, you will join your father's business."

In fact Andros had an academic background on his mother's side and was thinking more in terms of a doctorate. They would often use a Greek word, *morphosis*, which was to do with enlightenment.

Coming three years behind Andros, brother Evros retains vivid memories of the Stakis household at Aytoun Road, a typically big family house with people coming and going all the time and the inevitable queues for the bathroom in the morning. The four girls took a motherly interest in little Evros but manners had to be maintained in the Stakis household and the boys were expected to give their seats to the girls.

Only those ready and waiting at the door were likely to get a run to school in father's car, though the Rolls-Royce was a mixed blessing to Evros. He would insist on being dropped at Kelvinbridge, instead of the Academy gates, because of jealousy about his wealthy background.

Evros shares the Andros view about bigotry at Glasgow Academy. It was there, from the age of twelve, that he became acutely aware of differences. "I felt as a black boy would feel—and I hated it," is what he remembers. "Until the Pakistanis began to arrive, I was the darkest skin they had seen, me with my Mediterranean features. I was called a Paki and sometimes I was called Sambo and even in rugby games I have the scars to show the rougher treatment I received."

Evros was good at rugby and sport in general. Mercifully, he also had a sense of humour to cope with the teacher who called him T-bone, presumably after a steak from a Stakis restaurant! The consolation for a boy with such exotic good looks was that he was highly popular with the girls, not that that improved his popularity with the boys.

Nevertheless he can still recall going to a party at a girl's house and not being allowed over the doorstep because of his dark skin. Some time later, when the mother discovered that he was the son of Reo Stakis, he was invited with open arms. To his credit, Evros had the courage to tell the lady, very calmly, where to go!

If the two boys had their problems at Glasgow Academy, just off Great Western Road, the four girls were having a better time of it just a short distance away at Laurel Bank School for Girls, on Lilybank Terrace. While Rena and Ridi were more disciplined, paying attention to the teacher, Niki and Stassia saw themselves as more daring, even rebellious.

Rena and Niki were in the Hannan Watson house, both keen on sport and popular for their many contributions to school life. They were singers and dancers and took part in musical shows put on for the benefit of the war veterans at Erskine Hospital.

Niki was in the Laurel Bank School hockey team at a very young age and was particularly known as a high jumper and gymnast among her many sporting talents. Like the boys, she was not unaware of the racial differences—her skin was the darkest in the school at that time—and the girls would comment on her eyes and long eyelashes, so much so that she contemplated cutting those beautiful lashes.

But with her widespread popularity and devastating good looks, it was perhaps inevitable that Niki would stir jealousy. She had no sooner won an award at school and was being warmly congratulated by her many friends than she opened her desk and found that some girl had left a message: Greeks go home!

That incident devastated her. But loyal friends gathered round, formed their suspicions of who was responsible and got to the bottom of it. The culprit was a girl whose parents evidently disliked the Stakis family. She herself was an unpleasant and unpopular character and became the victim of her own rather sad little ploy.

Like many people from immigrant families, Niki felt the need to prove herself in this country and became so aware of the conflict in her dual culture that she would later take it as the thesis of her university course. Despite the inner divisions, she also felt at home in both Scotland and Cyprus so the conclusion of her study was that she was a citizen of the world.

But if there were difficulties for the youngsters, Niki sympathised with their parents, as Greeks trying to bring up their children in Scotland. They were so strict that she was unable to go out with boys until she went to university.

As the eldest daughter, Rena was first to experience a certain amount of repression, though the overall memory is of a happy childhood at Aytoun Road. As young girls, they were not allowed to go dancing in Glasgow. Involvement with boys was really taboo. With the best of intentions, Reo and Annitsa were upholding a Greek tradition which was to do with honour and the creating of a good impression. Greek sayings crept into much of their culture and one of them was to the effect that it is better to have your eye removed than your honour.

The Stakis children looked up to their father as a man of honour, knowing that his word was his promise and that he would never let them down. Rena was to reflect in later life that she had judged other people by those same standards, only to find that that was a big mistake. She had not been prepared to cope with the other sort.

Not that the Stakis girls were entirely biddable to the traditions of their race. Rena became quite a rebel, if not exactly a Hippy at least an independent spirit, singing the songs of freedom which were so much the rage of the 1960s. With as much respect as possible, she was trying to tell her parents, in her best Joan Baez and Bob Dylan style, that times were indeed a-changing.

If you were a doer like Rena, any attempt to restrict freedom ran contrary to nature and therefore to life itself. So she was consciously trying to change not only the attitude within the family but within the Greek community in this country as well. The normal practice of that community, right up to her parents' generation as we have seen, was for the male members of the family to arrange the marriages of the females. If that was to persist in the Beatles' generation, clearly there was going to be conflict.

9

FIRES AND RUMOURS

In that immediate post-war period from 1946 until 1951 Reo Stakis not only opened a dozen restaurants but was paying attention to the ancillaries as well. He bought the bakery business of Fred J. Malcolm at 444 Argyle Street, Glasgow, and expanded it into a chain of twenty-four bakery shops. Then came James Campbell and Son, a firm which had twelve Scotch ovens at Armour Street, Bridgeton.

"I was now very confident in what I was doing," was how he recalled his mood at that time. He was also more confident in his joustings with Izzy Walton, which had not gone away. Stakis had formed a property company called Ravenstone which had a site in Bearsden intended for a supermarket.

Walton came to challenge with a site on the other side of the town and both went after a licence. Only one would get it and, with another victory under his belt, Stakis knew that he had more than squared the account.

He was now well into the swing of borrowing money and paying it back. How else could you finance your business? As long as your judgement remained sound, the lenders would retain their belief in your ability to repay. It was just an added bonus to have a friend like Sir John Erskine who was so well acquainted with your methods from those early days on the doorstep.

But the money didn't always have to come from the bank. Settling down from that first burst of expansion, Reo Stakis found himself being introduced to one of the largest drinks companies in the country, Scottish Brewers, which would become even bigger under the name of Scottish and Newcastle.

There is always a catalyst in situations like this and the man who brokered the contact between Stakis and the brewers was George Preston, an Ayrshire businessman who had been observing his progress. He assured Sir William Younger, the brewery boss, that this Cypriot fellow was going places. "You should back him," was the advice. Sir William paid attention—and did.

Stakis was still in a small way at the time, but he wanted to buy pubs and Younger agreed to accommodate him by providing low-interest loans. It would go without saying that he would trade with the company but Stakis didn't seem to realise that that meant selling Sir William's beer and, when it became clear after six months that he was not doing so, the brewers decided to call off the loan.

George Preston intervened once more to say they would be making a big mistake. The position was clarified and never again did they have cause to complain about their new customer. It was the beginning of a long and valued business liaison which worked to the advantage of both sides.

Their arrangement was, roughly, that Stakis would open new pub-restaurants, build them up and sell them on to the brewery company. The selling-on price would be the turnover of the establishment.

Sir William Younger was soon passing over the Stakis connection to Peter Balfour, the man who would eventually succeed him as chairman of Scottish and Newcastle. Balfour had completed an army career in the mid-1950s and joined the McEwan company in Edinburgh.

Those great Scottish brewery families of McEwan and Younger were actually related and the union was strengthened in business when they came together as Scottish Brewers. As it happened, Peter Balfour gained his own private link into the system when Sir William Younger married his sister!

Stakis was deeply impressed by the new man, who struck him as being honest and straightforward. The respect was mutual, Balfour later recalling: "My boss used to say that, in business, honesty was a comparative term. That certainly did not apply to Reo. It was difficult in those days to get licences in Glasgow but Reo could always manage it. Those who didn't succeed in that way were jealous of him and spread all sorts of tales about how he got them.

"I don't believe they were true because I found him to be absolutely straightforward and extremely imaginative in his ideas. He was the first person for example to put down carpets in Scottish public houses. And he built big pubs, like the Dalriada in Glasgow, setting new standards in type and class from what we had known in Scotland. He was away ahead of his time. He also had a splendid architect in Tom Miller, who gave his premises a distinctive atmosphere."

George Preston was not the only man to cotton on to the potential of Reo Stakis. An up-and-coming Edinburgh lawyer, Charles Fraser, was representing the Forte organisation at licensing courts around Glasgow and Paisley when he became conscious of this newcomer who was managing to acquire so many licences. Consulting another lawyer, he was told: "Watch that man. He's going places."

Fraser not only watched him but came to know this fascinating little Cypriot, though little did he expect there would come a day when he had a crucial part to play in the fortunes of his business empire.

For all the progress, the Stakis profile was still comparatively modest at the start of the so-called Swinging Sixties, a decade when much would happen to change the social climate of Britain. Employment levels would reach that optimum point, amid widespread and unprecedented affluence, before automation began to threaten jobs.

However the fates arrange it, there was a sudden burst of rebellious energy, student protest, emancipation of youth, long hair, short skirts, Carnaby Street, Mary Quant—and all linked in a popular culture symbolised by the music of The Beatles. All eyes were on swinging Britain.

With new levels of spending and habits of eating out, Reo Stakis was planning his strategy for expansion into the hotel and leisure industry. There were modest developments like the Sans Souci at the top of Glassford Street, in the heart of Glasgow, in which he gave a £60,000 refurbishment to a restaurant which had first opened as far back as 1791.

It was one of the properties which would eventually be sold on to the brewers and when that moment arrived, Stakis realised once again how much he could trust Peter Balfour. Having stated the selling price he thought appropriate, he was reminded of the turnover arrangement by Mr Balfour, who pointed out that he was selling himself short.

The brewery boss insisted on paying the higher price, a gesture which was not forgotten at a later stage when Stakis needed to raise some cash and decided the time had come to sell his Princes Restaurant, the one which had figured in the battle with Izzy Walton.

The Princes was selling a lot of beer and was of immediate interest to Scottish and Newcastle. Over lunch with Peter Balfour in Edinburgh, Reo agreed to a price of £300,000 and returned to Glasgow feeling well pleased with his day. Back at the Princes, however, he was met by his lawyer, Hugh McCalman, and accountant William Duncan, who knew all the ramifications of the Stakis business, including the debts.

"We have great news," they chorused. "We have a buyer for the Princes."

"I'm sorry," said Reo, "but I have just sold the place."

"How much?"

"I got £300,000 from Scottish and Newcastle."

"But we have an offer for £70,000 more than that!"

His advisers argued the folly of turning down the higher offer till Reo was perspiring. But he had shaken hands on the deal and there was no changing his mind. It may have had no legal binding but it was a gentlemen's agreement and, if for no other reason, he owed that to Peter Balfour.

It was certainly a temptation, since the banks were pressing for repayments and the extra £70,000 would have been more than useful. But that was the end of the argument and William Duncan turned away in disbelief.

So Scottish and Newcastle became the new owners of The Princes but asked Reo Stakis to continue in the management role. Ironically, just a few days after the sale in December 1961, the restaurant went on fire. Restored to normality, there was another calamity in the following May when four hundred people had to flee the "Roast Chicken Fire" as it was called, with flames spreading through the entire block, causing serious damage to the Princes, the Pacific and the Copacabana. And as if that were not enough, the Princes hit the headlines a year later when it was reported to have had its third fire in sixteen months.

If this indicated the constant fire hazard in the kitchens of catering establishments, it also fuelled the rumours which engulfed Reo Stakis, despite the stout defence of the man put up by people like Peter Balfour.

Those rumours ranged from the fact that he seemed to get licences when nobody else could get them, to the suggestion that a number of fires in Stakis premises might have come under the classification of "insurance jobs." The inference of the former stories was that he must be giving out backhanders to people in authority, a suggestion which he meets head-on and laughs aside, pointing out that he merely persevered.

If he failed once, he would apply again and again. He would appear personally if necessary to press the justification of a claim and his theory was that, if that claim had enough substance, the chances were he would eventually get the licence.

"There is no greasing of palms," he said in self-defence. "I don't use any hocus-pocus in getting what I want and there is nothing underhand about it. People hear about the sites and licences we do acquire but they don't hear of the hundreds we don't get."

Nor did he underestimate the value of his lawyer at the time, Hugh McCalman, whose persuasive manner in front of the authorities did no harm in securing licences.

On the hint of possible arson, Reo Stakis was equally aware of the rumours and no less amused by their persistence, despite the serious and slanderous nature of the accusations. He had at least one first-hand experience of public gossip, on the day of that major outbreak at the Princes.

As the firemen fought the blaze he was standing, anonymously in the crowd across the street, with George Preston, the business-man who introduced him to Sir William Younger, when he heard one voluble onlooker declare to the crowd: "There's that so-and-so Stakis at it again. Another fire. How does he get away with it?" Even putting the morality of the argument aside, Reo Stakis points out that, from a purely practical angle, a fire is not a paying proposition!

At a later date, the rumours were rife when he was said to have offered £10,000 to clean up the environment surrounding Bingham's Pond, just off Great Western Road, at a time he was planning an extension to his nearby Pond Hotel. This was seen as a lever towards gaining permission. When the matter was inves-tigated, it turned out that Glasgow Corporation had actually invited him to make such a contribution as part of the development. So the hint of corruption had no foundation.

When confronted with the accusations, Stakis put the rumour-mongering down to jealousy among people who resented his success. "You have to be above getting upset by stories like that," he said. "If you listened to the inferences, you would never get anywhere in business."

When the records are examined, there has been a substantial body of applications turned down but he always forged ahead on the basis of a percentage of success. And there were times when you could turn failure into success. He once set out to buy a farm at Baillieston, on the fringe of Glasgow, with the hope of building a hotel. Having already acquired some land from Findlay Clark, the gardening people, he needed more space and pursued the owner of the adjoining property, which was Springhill Farm.

The farmer told him sternly: "I have dozens of people like you coming about here. But I'm not selling!" His family had been there since 1798 and he had no intention of breaking the bonds of nearly two hundred years for any fancy hotelier who happened to come along.

Reo Stakis knew when he was beaten and backed off. But soon there was a knock on his door. The farmer had had time to think about it and, for some reason best known to himself, might be prepared to sell after all. Was Mr Stakis still interested?

"Tell me this," said Stakis. "Of all the people who came after your farm, why did you come back to me?"

"Well," said the farmer, "I have a friend who is a friend of Lord Birsay, the High Court judge. He tells me that you too are a friend of Lord Birsay. And if you are a friend of Lord Birsay you are good enough for me."

Perhaps farming wasn't doing so well but, whatever his motives, he accepted exactly the same price as Mr Stakis had offered before. The deal was done but the farm was part of a green area and planning permission was still a hurdle to be cleared.

Reo Stakis still smiles about the court hearing when his case was being considered. He and the farmer were sitting together, follow-

ing the proceedings, when someone whispered in the latter's ear—
and he vanished. Had he perhaps had a change of heart? When he
reappeared in court some time later, Reo asked what had happened. "Oh, one of my cows was calving!" he announced audibly.

The outcome of this case, rather confounding the rumour-
mongers, was that planning permission was refused. But Reo Stakis
had a solution. The lace-man turned hotelier would now become
a farmer, building up a herd of milking cows, enrolling the skills
of his chef at the Ivy Restaurant—and producing a high-quality
yoghurt. There was always a way out. And when Springhill Farm
was eventually sold it became a business park.

10

SCOTLAND THE BRAVE

As the momentum of the Sixties gathered pace, Reo had already built up a chain of thirty eating houses, hotels and bars throughout central Scotland. Outwith Glasgow, he was turning the Splendid Restaurant in Hamilton into a hotel and had plans for Stirling, Dundee, Motherwell and Kilmacolm as well as Edinburgh, the city which had so intrigued him when he first set foot in Scotland in the late 1920s.

As the empire grew, there was one drawback to public houses: There was no Sunday opening in Scotland. In order to sell drink on the Sabbath you had to qualify as a hotel but that was a simple challenge for the enterprising Reo, who turned his attention to small establishments of four or five bedrooms, which met the requirement.

It was on this basis that he entered the business of running hotels for which the name of Stakis would yet become famous. Having opened one in Bearsden and one in the Shawlands district of Glasgow, his next move was the purchase of a private house on Eastwoodmains Road, between Clarkston and Eastwood Toll, on the south side of the city, not far from a rival hotel which had become well-known as the Macdonald.

That private house was the nucleus of the Redhurst Hotel, which became one of the most popular haunts on the south side, in demand for weddings and other functions as well as for its public house facility. Apart from these district hotels, however, he was moving into the more prestigious end of the market.

In 1962 he was approached by a gentleman who had had a rather fortuitous inheritance from an uncle. It included a hotel on the Isle of Skye and the Birnam at Dunkeld as well as the imposing Dunblane Hydro and, while he intended to keep Dunkeld, he was offering the other two for sale. Reo Stakis was not interested in the island hotel but struck a deal on the Hydro, where the gentleman had apparently been running up losses. (That deal, incidentally, was completed in a lay-by on the Glasgow-Ayr road, which was certainly a more casual choice than the stuffiness of a boardroom.)

Reo Stakis could see the potential of the former spa, well situated on the hill, within the village boundary of Dunblane and with a considerable acreage which included the terraced lawns reaching towards the main road coming from Perth. With the ever-present threat of house-building, however, he further secured the privacy of his property when he bought the adjoining Ledcameroch House and grounds from a timber merchant, as well as another house called Holmhill.

These extra properties cost around £20,000 each, Ledcameroch becoming staff quarters for the Hydro while Holmhill fell victim to vandals and had to be pulled down. Dunblane Hydro was now enclosed in nearly forty acres but the place itself was in a run-down state.

Reo took a personal hand in bringing his new acquisition up to standard, moving in to stay for several weeks and discovering that the food was dreadful. It did not take long for an experienced hotelier to find what it needed. Good food and good service were usually the starting-points and within six months he had turned the loss into a profit.

Dunblane Hydro became a highly successful addition to the Stakis empire, employing up to 250 people and bringing extra trade to other businesses in the town. The hotel itself, with 150 bedrooms, heated swimming-pool, tennis courts and ballroom reached an occupancy rate of eighty per cent and drew clients of all nationalities as well as developing a lucrative business in conference bookings.

It was in such a lush and attractive setting that it became a jewel in the Stakis crown. In the modern manner, it needed a leisure centre and today Dunblane has the full complex, from tennis courts to gymnasium.

Not least of the assets at the Hydro was the full-time presence of Jim MacLeod and his band, who would become an institution at Dunblane. Jim, whose father was a local postman, had just signed a new recording contract with Decca and was already a household name, having reached a wider public through *The White Heather Club* on BBC Television. In his popular band show, he was able to introduce cabaret stars ranging from Roberto Cardinale and the Caribbean All-Steel Band to Scotland's own Anne and Laura Brand.

Proof of Jim MacLeod's enduring appeal lay in the fact that his piano-playing and whispering tenor voice were still delighting customers at Dunblane more than thirty years after he arrived. His Hogmanay Night parties continued to be among the great social occasions in the Scottish calendar and, with the Royal Family among his most ardent admirers, it was not surprising that, in 1998, he chalked up his 25th appearance as the provider of music at the annual Ghillies' Ball at Balmoral.

The old Grosvenor Hotel, at the corner of Glasgow's Great Western Road and Byres Road, was in a run-down condition with only a few rooms when Reo Stakis cast an eye over it and realised the potential of its prestigious site. It stood on the elegance of Grosvenor Terrace, a sweeping Victorian block which was subject to a preservation order, one of only four A-listed terraces in the city. The hotel itself was built in 1855 by J. T. Rochead to a Venetian design which is remarkable for its window formations.

After Reo bought the old Grosvenor in 1971 it lay empty and apparently deteriorating for two years. But he was also taking the opportunity to buy up flats along that terrace, opposite the Botanic Gardens, and when his plans were finally revealed they amounted to a large and classy hotel, which became a flagship of his organisation.

Even here, however, he was not to escape the horrors of fire. On the first Saturday of January, 1978, an outbreak in the kitchen of the grill room was soon engulfing the entire building and guests were fleeing for their lives.

To make matters worse, it happened in the middle of a firemen's strike and the blaze had to be tackled by sailors, soldiers and Royal Marine Commandos, with their distinctive "Green Goddess" vehicles, who had been brought in to cover the emergency.

Inevitably, their lack of experience prolonged the operation but, while the building was devastated, there was consolation in the fact that the precious façade remained standing. Surveying the ruins, Reo Stakis vowed that he would restore his beloved Grosvenor—and that is precisely what happened, to the extent that it continues to be one of Scotland's most attractive hostelries.

The pattern for bigger hotels was now established and others were soon to follow. Reo saw the need for a large one within easy reach of Glasgow Airport. He acquired the site he wanted by a complicated set of land deals, revealing the workings of a business mind which elude most of us.

His target was Renfrew Golf Club, to which he made the offer of building a new golf course in return for their property. He then bought another tract of adjoining land, sold some of it for housing and more of it for a development of those out-of-town megastores which would soon become the fashion. He had created a whole complex and was left with the desirable site, as he had first envisaged, for the building of his £750,000 Normandy Hotel, the most ambitious project to date for the Stakis organisation.

The choice of name has a romantic little tale of its own. When the architects Tom Miller and Partners were designing the building, ever conscious that it would need a name, someone had the wit to notice that the project file bore the serial number of 1066. The Battle of Hastings? That conflict was won by the Duke of Normandy, alias William the Conqueror—and that was how the Renfrew hotel got its name.

A more immediate battle threatened from an argument as to whether the name should end with an "ie" or a "y" but the matter was resolved when Mr Stakis stepped in to conduct an opinion poll, which said that the "y"s had it.

At Aytoun Road, Sundays were kept for the family and after church Reo and Annitsa would take the children for a drive. But there was no guarantee that the natural instinct for attractive building sites would be switched off. On one particular Sunday the democratic vote was to go either where there was the best ice-cream or the best sands. Reo remembered Nardini's ice-cream at Largs and off they set, skirting the Clyde estuary by Port Glasgow and Greenock.

They were driving along that attractive waterfront at Gourock when Reo spotted a site with a wonderful view. Even if business was intruding on the family outing, Annitsa had to agree that the site was most desirable.

"If I can build here, this hotel will be dedicated to you," said Reo to Annitsa, with a commendable dash of diplomacy. They reached Largs, enjoyed their ice-cream and the spectacular views of the Clyde—and next day Reo went off to see the Provost of Gourock, who was taken aback by the approach.

But he agreed with the concept, a licence was duly forthcoming and that was how the Gantock Hotel, on Gourock's glorious front, came into existence, duly dedicated to Annitsa. Reo recalled these origins when he went to the re-opening of the Gantock, refurbished in 1997, at a ceremony performed by the captain of the QE2.

The next target was Andrew Carnegie's home town of Dunfermline, where Reo Stakis wanted to convert an old school. Once again, the first call was a courtesy to the local provost, a lady who clearly had not caught up with the activities of Mr Stakis.

"Have you done anything like this before?" she wanted to know.

Well, yes, he wasn't exactly a novice. Would she like to see over Dunblane Hydro, for example? That was enough to convince the lady she was not dealing with some fly-by-night. And that was how Dunfermline landed its Belleville Hotel.

To help the tourist trade, the Labour Government returned to power in 1964 was offering an incentive of £1000 per bedroom for the building of hotels. But not even that kind of encouragement was enough to attract potential hoteliers to unfashionable places like Bradford, the industrial town in West Yorkshire which rather came into the "black hole" category of urban classification.

The local authority in Bradford had done its best to stir interest but to no avail. Stakis conferred with his architect and his managing director, John Loughray, and decided to take a look at the situation, starting with a courtesy call to the civic head, who turned out once more to be a lady. If this deal materialised, it would be the Scottish company's first venture into England.

The lady mayor prepared for their arrival and showed that Reo Stakis was not the only one with diplomacy in his locker. As the Scottish party arrived at the Town Hall in the centre of Bradford, the municipal bells were ringing out a melody which could be clearly identified as "Scotland The Brave"!

The smile which spread over their faces confirmed that the lady mayor of Bradford had set the proper mood. She compounded that with an impressive reception, after which she heaped much praise on the Scots.

Mr Stakis acknowledged the flattery but knew there was business to attend to. Yes, he was considering opening a hotel in Bradford but he would come to the point and present his terms for doing so. If they would give him planning permission and all the licences he wanted, he would promise to build a hotel.

They agreed to every request and he set out to build his 120-room hotel which, given the government subsidy, meant that he had a £120,000 start on a venture which would cost less than a million. It was good business for Stakis as well as for Bradford and the result was the city-centre Norfolk Gardens Hotel which remains in the company's hands to this day.

11

ENTER THE CHEVALIER

From lace to restaurants and hotels, Reo Stakis had established himself successfully on the Scottish business scene. But casinos had not entered his head. They had never been part of British life, more a pursuit of the profligate in places like Monte Carlo where men in dark glasses and big cigars, silent and mysterious, could make or lose vast fortunes in the dim-lit dens of gambling.

Casinos were even such a dirty word in some quarters that, when Stakis did eventually test the waters of the gaming world, one of his directors promptly resigned. But he had not even contemplated such an idea, which was in any case against the law, until an astute London barrister, studying the matter in the early 1960s, advised a client that he had found a loophole and reckoned it would be possible to operate within the law. Britain's first casino was thus opened in the Bayswater district of London.

Even then, it took a suggestion from a Stakis employee, a waiter called Panos Miltiadou, to sow the seed. Reo had first met Panos in London, later giving him a job in Glasgow and coming to know that he was a bit of a gambler.

"Why don't you open a casino?" asked Panos.

"I don't know anything about them," was the reply.

"You'll soon learn," he said.

Reo had recently taken over the old Naafi Club at the top of

Buchanan Street, which had closed because of the reduced number of Servicemen in the area and had been lying empty. This would become the headquarters of the Stakis organisation but there was room for a lot more than that.

The idea of a casino was now working in his mind and public curiosity was first aroused by a newspaper advertisement in London and France, seeking a casino manager for Glasgow at a salary of £9000 plus commission, and a head croupier at £7000.

All was revealed in February 1964 when Reo Stakis announced his most spectacular plan to date. Having already encouraged the Scots to eat out, he was now embracing the social mood of the Swinging Sixties and opening a plush established called the Chevalier, which would offer the combination of dinner, dancing and cabaret—with Britain's biggest and most luxurious casino on the floor above.

All this would be housed in the new premises in Buchanan Street, roughly where the Glasgow Royal Concert Hall stands today. The head croupier, M. Jean Beysson, a Frenchman who had been lured from London, was already in place and there would be room for about five hundred private members in the new casino, paying fees between three and five guineas per year.

The Chevalier opened its doors to the public on Wednesday, 17th June, 1964, after a more private champagne reception on the previous evening to which several hundred guests were invited. They had the first chance to see the plush set-up, with that dining-cum-cabaret room on the first floor, capable of holding up to 250 diners. A feature of these spectacular surroundings was a circular dance-floor of glass with lights filtering up from below. Glasgow had not seen anything quite like this.

Carpets of red, green and grey would admirably set off the beautiful gold silk of the curtains and the pale green of the walls and those first guests were deeply impressed by what they saw.

In counterpoint to the candlelit dinners with soft music and top cabaret acts there was the quiet tension of the casino, roulette wheels spinning merrily under the gaze of familiar tycoons, some of them millionaires who had gambled all the way from Monte Carlo to Las Vegas and said this was one of the best they had seen.

The Chevalier caused a big stir on Glasgow's social scene and once again Reo Stakis had led the way in showing how an increasingly affluent society could spend its leisure time and money.

The resident musicians were Peggy O'Keefe and her Quartet, the vivacious and highly-talented Peggy having recently arrived from her native Australia to become a big hit in Scotland as a pianist and entertainer. The star attraction in the first week at the Chevalier was a popular singer of the day, Ronnie Carroll, better known to some as the husband of an even bigger name in the Sixties, Millicent Martin.

So the Chevalier was up and running, with a major burst of publicity and widespread interest and with many a star-studded night in store. The legality of the gambling element in such establishments was still something of a grey area, despite the confidence of that London barrister.

But it came a good deal clearer on a summer night of 1964 when calamity struck and a question-mark was placed over the whole future of the Chevalier. Just before midnight on Saturday, 8th August, fourteen uniformed policemen stormed the plush nightclub and brought a stunned silence to an elegant clientèle as they sealed off the gaming rooms and began interviewing the 300 people in the building.

As some raced for the exits, they were stopped by the police who had brought along a Black Maria, a well-known police vehicle of the time, and were confiscating the roulette wheels and any other moveable equipment of the gambling scene. Popular comedian of the day Jimmy Logan had just driven up in his Rolls-Royce and was alarmed by all the activity, not least since his famous sister, jazz singer Annie Ross, was the cabaret attraction that week.

Reo Stakis was in London at the time, totally unaware of the drama being enacted at his Glasgow casino. The focus of attention fell on people like 52-year-old Panayiotis Panos, the casino manager, and chief croupier Jean Beysson, 60, who were technically in charge. An irony of the police raid was that one of their superiors, James Lyon, had recently resigned as CID boss of the Marine Division to become security boss of the casino!

While the legal position of gaming in Britain remained in doubt, the justification for the raid was to do with a technicality about the fairness of play. The allegation was that the odds of winning were not equally favourable to the players and the house and that the game was therefore not being conducted according to the conditions of the Betting, Gaming and Lotteries Act of 1963.

When four of the senior staff appeared in Glasgow Sheriff Court on the Monday morning, it emerged that the police were acting on complaints from the boss of a rival casino. The Chief Constable had received a letter from Robert Jones of Clarence Drive, Glasgow, who was connected with the Club St Tropez in Wellington Street. After visiting the Chevalier in June, Mr Jones said he had instructed his solicitor to write the letter.

Mr Gordon Stott, defending, asked Mr Jones if it was true he had made threats to Mr Stakis regarding the opening of his club. Jones replied: "I never spoke to him in my life until that time at the Chevalier." He denied writing an anonymous letter to Mr Stakis to say he should not open his club. Another letter of complaint had been received from a Finlay McNaughton of Drumchapel, who was questioned as to whether he was merely a cat's paw. He agreed that he had never actually been in the Chevalier and that the letter had been typed by a friend he met in a city pub. As far as he could gather, the roulette at the casino was not being run fairly as far as the player was concerned. He denied that someone had put him up to writing the letter and said he did it on the spur of the moment.

A mathematics lecturer at Glasgow University, Dr Alexander Robertson, was asked to give an opinion about the fairness of the system. Conceding that he knew nothing about roulette, he ventured the view that the game as played gave a slight advantage to the "bank."

Jean Beysson, the croupier, said he had worked at all the main casinos in Europe and had been the first to introduce roulette to London. He claimed that the game and the odds at the Chevalier were exactly the same as those offered in London and in France, except that in France the bank was always held by the house.

In Britain, at every spin of the wheel the players were given the opportunity to take the bank if they wished, giving them an additional advantage over gamblers in the top casinos of Europe.

"When the Chevalier opened, everyone wanted to play the bank," he smiled. "But after a while, they all wanted to play against it."

Sheriff Francis Middleton found two of the croupiers not guilty. They were Fivos Scholarios, 32, of Maxwell Drive, Pollokshields, and 21-year-old Aris Arestis, a student of Lilybank Gardens, Hillhead, who was studying engineering in Glasgow and had taken the casino job to make some extra money. He was the son of a senior police officer in Greece.

Sheriff Middleton continued the case against manager Panos and croupier Beysson, saying it merited more legal consideration than he could give it there and then. At a later date, however, he found them guilty of running an unlawful game of roulette but gave Beysson a complete discharge, while fining Panos a total of fifty pounds.

The sheriff agreed with defence counsel that it had been in the nature of a test case in this country. He was satisfied that every endeavour had been made to run the club on reasonable lines so he was not imposing unnecessary punishment for what appeared to be no more than a mistake in the circumstances.

Reo Stakis gave an assurance that the casino would be operated one hundred per cent according to the sheriff's judgement. When asked by the sheriff what the consequences of the findings would be, Mr Gordon Stott said the bank would have to be offered more openly. If that were not economically possible then the club would have to come to an end.

The Chevalier survived, however, as a casino as well as a top restaurant. It is interesting in hindsight to find that journalists were commenting on the fact that men were now taking their wives on an evening out—and that they were drinking with their meals.

Holidays abroad were coming into fashion and Reo Stakis was further changing the social habits of Scotland by pushing for later licensing hours in which the ordinary citizen could relax over a meal and a bottle of wine. The Chevalier therefore became a popular haunt for late-night people, whether they were there for the food, drink and cabaret or were drawn into the mystique of the gaming rooms.

12

NIGHT OF THE STARS

The Chevalier soon established itself on the Glasgow social scene as a place for a good night out, where people went to see and to be seen. It was new, it was glamorous and exciting, much in the mood of the decade, and Reo Stakis retained the memory of a particularly pleasurable evening when he danced at the Chevalier with Princess Margaret.

Earlier that evening in February 1966 the Princess had flown into Glasgow for a glittering "Night of the Stars" in Jimmy Logan's Metropole Theatre at St George's Cross. The crowds lining the streets to welcome the royal visitor included large numbers of American sailors in town, curious to see what this fascination with the royals was all about.

The Princess, dressed in a full-length coral silk gown, was greeted at the theatre door by Jimmy Logan and Lord Provost John Johnston and soon entered into the spirit of the show, a charity event for Dr Barnardo's Homes, which was co-produced by Logan and the programme director at Scottish Television, Francis Essex.

After a fanfare of trumpets, Princess Margaret had scarcely settled into the flower-decked royal box than the audience, led by comedian Jack Radcliffe, burst into the local anthem, "I Belong to Glasgow." The programme ranged from Una McLean's recollections of a tenement childhood (jeely pieces, hot peas and mammy at the jawbox) to Stanley Baxter's "Sammy McBride, Pride of the Guards," on duty outside Buckingham Palace. (Telephone number: Busby 6634!)

The entertainment included Millicent Martin, Dickie Henderson, Grace Clark and Colin Murray, and Bill Simpson, the former Scottish Television announcer who became Dr Finlay in the popular TV series. All that plus the United States Third Air Force Band, which came all the way from Germany for the occasion. Princess Margaret was thoroughly enjoying herself, making it known to Francis Essex, however, that she was glad it was not an all-Scottish entertainment. "You can get too much of the kilt and haggis, can't you?" was her comment.

After the show, Reo Stakis hosted a late-night supper for two hundred people at the Chevalier and led the Princess to the dance-floor where she became so caught up in the mood of the night that she asked if the Peggy O'Keefe Quartet could play beyond their time. She was still dancing at 2am. Though the cabaret room was naturally closed to the public, that did not apply to the casino upstairs, where the serious business of pursuing that elusive fortune proceeded apace, well into the smoky depths of early morning.

That gala night was by no means the first time that Reo Stakis had quietly played a highly generous hand in the name of charity. Jimmy Logan remembered how he and Jack Radcliffe and several other top entertainers had decided something should be done for spastics, at a time when that word had scarcely reached the vocabulary. Jimmy suggested they should call it "Stars Organisation for Spastics," a view not shared by some of his colleagues.

However they decided to take over the famous Alhambra Theatre in the centre of Glasgow for a full week's show on behalf of the charity. Apart from the money raised, Jimmy Logan still believes that one of their main achievements was in making the word "spastic" acceptable.

The show would be on a lavish scale and in order to cut down costs the artistes would give their services free and not even expect too much in the way of hospitality. They assembled a cast of 250 people, including Scotland's top entertainers, along with pipe bands and choirs. Richard Hearne, better known as Mister Pastry, came up from London and for the finale they managed to entice Olive Gilbert, a famous contralto of the day who was best remembered from the great Ivor Novello musicals at Drury Lane.

In view of the frugal hospitality, Jimmy Logan phoned Reo Stakis to ask if he might lay on a modest tea for the cast after the shows. But Reo was determined to do more than that for the charity. He called back to say he would like to offer them a drink as well but the licensing authorities were not likely to believe that a cast of 275 were his friends. There would be difficulty about a special licence.

Jimmy Logan phoned the home of Sir Myer Galpern, Lord Provost of Glasgow, and explained the problem to Lady Galpern. She was back on the phone within twenty minutes to say she had been in touch with the Chief Constable and his reply had been: "Go ahead—with my compliments!"

Whereas it was intended for the Princes Restaurant, Reo Stakis expanded it to his Ca'dora building in Renfield Street and it was not so much a five-shilling tea he laid on for the stars as a four-course dinner with drinks. Everyone was delighted. Nor was this a one-off occasion. He proceeded to repeat the hospitality in succeeding years as Jimmy Logan and his friends continued with their Stars for Spastics extravaganzas.

Jimmy Logan had taken over the Metropole in a bid to sustain the variety theatre in Scotland, and sought to run it on a commercial footing even when the business was having a rough patch. For all his sterling efforts, Jimmy ran into bad times, losing his theatre and most of his money. He was later to reveal that his bank balance was down to about £200.

A newspaper article made it clear that the popular comedian

and member of the Logan Family show, who first gained fame in the 1949 film *Floodtide*, had reached a low ebb in his fortunes. As so often in life, it was at that nadir in his career that Jimmy discovered his real friends.

But he hardly expected the call which came to his dressing-room when he was making the film *Carry on Abroad*. It was from Reo Stakis, saying "Jimmy, you must be under a lot of pressure. I just want you to know there is a personal cheque here for whatever you need—Five thousand? Ten thousand?"

Jimmy was overwhelmed by the generosity and only his pride persuaded him to turn down the offer. In all truth, he could well have been doing with the money but he had to say he was all right. The gesture was never forgotten.

Like many another, Logan simply marvelled at how Mr Stakis had come to a strange country and established himself so successfully from such a modest beginning. For a quiet and humble little man, he had become a giant on the business and social scene of Scotland.

13

REO ESCAPES THE MAFIA

If Reo Stakis claimed that he never did come to know anything
about gambling, he did understand very promptly that casinos
were good business, all the more profitable for dealing in cash.
The Stakis empire had soon built a chain of more than twenty of
them, spreading to East Kilbride and the basement of Dunblane
Hydro, as well as to Kilmacolm Hydro. Not least, he had negotiated successfully with Mrs Waldock and her affluent family who
owned the Imperial Hotel in Russell Square, London, and was
thus able to storm the capital by opening the very plush Regency
Casino in that popular square.

But where there is gambling there is likely to be the Mafia, in
one or other of its forms. The British scene was no exception and
when the first casino opened in London's Bayswater there were
doubts about the owner, another Cypriot called Demetriou. He
was later killed in a car crash in what were regarded as suspicious
circumstances.

The matter of underworld influence gained much publicity when
the well-known Hollywood film star George Raft was all set to
host a night club and casino in Berkeley Square, London. Reo
Stakis did happen to see Raft in London but the film star's stay
was limited once the immigration authorities discovered his presence.

There had long been suspicions about George Raft and his connections with the Mafia in the United States. His Hollywood career had begun, it was said, when he was providing young muscle in the protection racket and found himself being offered a small role in the 1929 movie *Queen of the Night Clubs*.

There followed a series of gangster parts before he was signed up by Paramount and graduated to leading man in Mae West's first film, *Night After Night*, in 1932. He moved to Warner Brothers and became a big name, nevertheless turning down *Casablanca*, *The Maltese Falcon* and *High Sierra*, thus proving if nothing else that he didn't have the wit of the brooding Bogart, who starred in all three. It was Raft's rejection of *High Sierra* which gave Bogie his first big break.

But his name became tarnished and the underworld reputation never left him. That was why, in that attempt to work in London in the 1960s, he was refused permission. The Government was cracking down on the potential for crime in the casinos and Reo Stakis believed that if they had not done so, Britain would have been in the grip of one of the biggest Mafia operations in the world.

He himself narrowly escaped their influence. In an industry which was so new to this country, he had decided to operate a school for croupiers, training twenty people at a time. In search of the right man to run it, he was introduced to an American gent who impressed him as the man for the job. He welcomed him to his home in Pollokshields and in their preliminary discussions there were plans for his children to gain entry to the same upmarket schools in Glasgow as the Stakis children.

Before the matter was finalised, however, Reo Stakis came across a newspaper report from America which revealed that the man he had earmarked for the teaching of his young croupiers was none other than a leading figure in the American Mafia!

Fortunately, the Government brought in Sir Stanley Raymond

to regularise the gambling scene in Britain, bringing it within the law and clamping down on the gangster element. Raymond was strict but fair and there is no doubt that his diligence was responsible for Britain having the best-run casinos in the world.

The Stakis organisation continued to profit from this business and, when Ladbroke lost licences through contravention of the law, it stepped in and bought five of their establishments for £4.4 million.

As the business continued to expand and prosper, so did individual careers develop, sometimes quite unexpectedly, as in the case of Frances Timoney, who found herself in the role of private secretary to Reo Stakis, having followed in the footsteps of Jean Mitchell and Alexis Macbeath.

Frances had grown up in the Muirend district of Glasgow, set aside her ambition to be a vet and trained as a secretary before joining the famous Anchor Line in St Vincent Place. In the 1950s there was still the bustle of the maritime world down there on Yorkhill Quay, where the young girl would see life in all its shades.

Ships were still leaving the Clyde for exotic parts like India and her mettle would be tested on Hogmanay Night when it was part of her job to round up seamen from quayside pubs to board ship for the New York departure.

Frances spent a further seven years with the industrial catering side of Trust House before answering a box number in the *Glasgow Herald*. Little did she know it would shape the rest of her life. From that day in 1968 she would be personal assistant to Mr Stakis, a close witness and confidante of a man already well-known for his Glasgow restaurants and due to become an even bigger name in the hotel and leisure industry of this country.

Frances Timoney still remembers the early excitement of her daily routine, turning up every morning at the Parliamentary Road headquarters of the Stakis organisation, at that time a modest operation in which the leading names were John Loughray as general manager, Tony Lang as company secretary, and Don Cornock, a former Scottish professional footballer, as finance director.

It was a novel experience for a young Glasgow woman to be mounting the stairs to the third floor of that building which also housed the Chevalier and finding that gamblers from the night before were still in the second-floor casino at breakfast time, engrossed in their poker games.

All was silent on the first floor, where the nightclub activities of the Chevalier were now but a memory of dim-lit dining and dancing and warm romance, lingering still in a suggestive cocktail of stale nicotine and perfume perspired. Working for Reo Stakis, Frances would soon discover, was no nine-to-five routine. Since he himself did not follow such strictures, he did not expect his loyal lieutenants to be any different.

So, as Frances Timoney settled into a career which would see her through the rest of her working life, she adjusted quite happily to the fact that, as the boss's right hand, she would be working not only beyond the hours of the day but turning up at weekends when required.

In 1970, she was among those who were reminded that nothing stands still for ever. The Chevalier had created a new kind of glamour in Glasgow's night life, bringing some of the greatest names in showbusiness, from Matt Monro to Cleo Laine, and beaming a live cabaret show to the nation in *Night Club Night*.

Others had tried to follow the example but found it so expensive that their clubs closed within a short time of opening. The social mood was changing again and there came a point when Mr Stakis announced that even he could no longer afford to bring up the top stars from London.

So the Chevalier as we had known it closed its doors in July 1970 and re-opened as a different kind of restaurant. There were also changes in the gaming laws that year, bringing closure to many casinos in this country, including the one at Dunblane Hydro. The Chevalier moved its casino to Hope Street, opposite the Central Hotel, and was still there in the 1990s, along with the Regency in Waterloo Street and the Princes at Charing Cross.

The Kilmacolm Hydro had been a particular disappointment. Built in 1883 as a hydropathic hotel, it became famous for its soft water which was said to cure aches and pains of all kinds. The rich came from all over the world to fill the hundred bedrooms with an occupancy rate to raise envy today.

Reo bought it in 1963 but could get a licence for serving drink only with a meal. He turned it into the first casino in Renfrewshire but, still with no licence, decided to close it in 1969. The hurricane of the previous year caused widespread damage and the famous old hotel was pulled down and the site given over to housing.

The casinos were not delivering to their potential in the mid-nineties and all twenty-two, from Gibraltar to the Isle of Man, became the subject of a major review. In 1996 the company opened the rather spectacular Riverboat Casino on Clydeside and followed with an equally successful Maybury in Edinburgh a year later, with four more of similar character on the way. The Riverboat enrolled 30,000 new members in its first year.

14

TOWARDS AVIEMORE

Like all good businessmen, Reo Stakis knew that, whatever your own abilities, the greatest skill of all was to surround yourself with the right people and then give them leadership. The triumphs and later turbulence of the Stakis organisation involved an intriguing collection of lieutenants who could not have dreamed what lay in store as they made their individual ways into the company.

Their collective experience is a substantial part of the Reo Stakis story. The first of the key figures to arrive on the scene had been John Loughray, who grew up in the Knightswood district of Glasgow, son of a shipyard worker at Yarrow's on the Clyde. After Hillhead High, he went to the Scottish Hotel School at Crookston, did his National Service and entered his chosen profession in Fife before heading for the old-established Athenaeum Restaurant in Aberdeen.

It was in 1960 that he moved back south to join Reo Stakis, who was still at an early stage in building his catering empire. First stop was the Sans Souci in Glassford Street, Glasgow, before taking over as manager at the Garrion Hotel in Motherwell. Proving his capabilities, he took on a kind of troubleshooting role as an area manager and had to sort out problems at the Invercarse Hotel, Dundee, before assuming the prestigious post of manager at the Dunblane Hydro.

In 1967 he was back at headquarters in Glasgow at a time when the company was developing rapidly, encouraged by that Government incentive of £1000 per room for creating new hotels.

Loughray saw himself expanding with the company, a tall, imposing figure who regarded Reo Stakis as a paternal influence, a man with whom he had a good rapport and who was appreciative of all his hard work. His rewards were not long in coming. By 1969 he was a director of the company, three years later he became assistant managing director and by 1976 he was managing director of the Stakis organisation at the age of forty-two.

"I was never one for jumping from job to job," he said. "Nor was there any need to do so. Mr Stakis and I got on very well together and I had a career progression."

Loughray observed the workings of the tycoon mind and knew that if there was one name bigger on the Scottish business scene than his own boss it was that of Sir Hugh Fraser, the dynamic entrepreneur who expanded the family store in Buchanan Street, Glasgow, into a major retail empire across Britain, crowning his achievements with the purchase of the prestigious Harrod's of London in 1959.

For his public work, he later became Lord Fraser of Allander, that service including his part in developing the Highland village of Aviemore, on the route from Perth to Inverness, into a major tourist centre. The Government of the day, appreciating his talent for making things work, gave him the go-ahead to lead what would be one of the biggest and most ambitious ventures Scotland had seen.

This would be a complex of hotels, shops and leisure facilities on that main north road, linked into the skiing possibilities and other mountain pursuits which were just being developed in that western area of the Cairngorms.

Other commercial interests were encouraged to cluster around Fraser's leadership and the business nose of Reo Stakis did not fail to sense the opportunity of an active involvement with the Aviemore project. He had thoughts of a hotel at the complex but there came a stage when he disagreed with some of the developments and decided to pull out.

Aviemore ran into bad publicity when its architect, John Poulson from Pontefract, was not only heading for bankruptcy but was jailed for corruption in the obtaining of contracts. A senior official at the Scottish Office, George Pottinger, went with him.

Reo Stakis did not entirely lose his interest in Aviemore, however. He merely stood back to study the situation. Quite separate from the Aviemore Centre but nearer to the mountains, the Rank Organisation owned the Coylumbridge Hotel, which stood where the whole complex had originally been intended.

Rank decided that its Highland hotel did not fit into the image and when Reo Stakis heard it was coming on the market, he gave John Loughray one of his early opportunities to negotiate. Loughray boarded the night train to London, grabbed a few hours in the sleeper and was on the doorstep of the Rank Organisation for a very early meeting with the managing director, who was already at his desk in what was once an exclusive London town house.

He never forgot that, mounting the stair, he was startled to be confronted by a massive bear, which happily turned out to be stuffed. Privately hoping this was not to be an omen, he regained equilibrium and before the normal breakfast hour had negotiated a purchase which took both the Coylumbridge and the Five Bridges Hotel at Gateshead into the ownership of Stakis.

The total buying price was £1.2 million but, considering they would sell on the Five Bridges for £700,000, it was a marvellous deal for the Scottish company, acquiring the Aviemore hotel for no more than £500,000.

The much-publicised Aviemore Centre, as guided into shape by Sir Hugh Fraser, eventually fell on hard times and Reo Stakis bought the entire complex for a mere £1 million in 1986. He would retain his admiration for Fraser as a successful businessman but felt he did not know enough about that kind of project.

"He meant well but he was the wrong man for that sort of role," he said. Thus the Stakis organisation acquired the Four Seasons and the Badenoch hotels, from which he was soon making money. Aviemore was heading for a major restoration towards the end of the century.

That earlier experience of conflict between Reo Stakis and Izzy Walton showed the kind of business infighting which can exist among those who cheerily greet each other in the conviviality of a coffee house. Despite his admiration for Hugh Fraser, Reo learned to have reservations about the same gentleman.

There was a time when they would meet for lunch every week, an occasion which would cause some private amusement because that midday meal of the fabulously wealthy Fraser would usually amount to a big roll and jam.

Since Stakis was always on the lookout for sites, he appreciated the fact that Fraser used to say: "Reo, if there is ever anything I can do to help . . ." One day there was. Reo had spotted a most desirable site with a magnificent view at Milngavie, in that up-market fringe of the Glasgow area not far from Fraser's residence at Mugdock. He understood it belonged to John Lawrence, prominent Scottish builder and chairman of Rangers Football Club; but Lawrence assured him it was Hugh Fraser's.

At the weekly lunch it would be a simple matter to test out the offer of help. Could he have that piece of land? "I'll think about it and tell you next week," said Fraser. On the following week he came fairly straight to the point. It could have sounded like a jocular response but it soon dawned on Stakis that it was deadly serious: "I bought that site to keep people like you away from there!"

Reo had intended to build a hotel at that Mugdock site but that was the end of that. "He was a strange man," was his controlled verdict.

He did acquire another site in that area, the 150 acres of Dougalston at Bearsden, the estate which nearly became the home of the Burrell Collection when Sir William agreed to it, even if it did not conform to his condition that it should be a certain distance from the smoke of Glasgow. Both of these schemes came unstuck, however, and Reo later built a pub-restaurant called The Stables.

When he bought the Glasgow Grosvenor on Great Western Road he was also negotiating, through his Ravenstone property company, to acquire some adjacent buildings round the corner, with the intention of putting up a supermarket on Byres Road. That brought him back in touch with the Fraser family—the premises had been occupied by Wylie and Lochhead—but no longer with Lord Fraser, who had died before his time in 1966.

Stakis was now dealing with the only son and namesake, who found himself unexpectedly in his father's chair while still in his twenties. It was young Hugh's first major deal, concluded to their mutual satisfaction, and Reo Stakis took an instant liking to the young man.

Like others who came to know this most personable of people, however, he grew increasingly concerned about his gambling addiction and, as the biggest casino owner in Scotland, made a special plea that he should not frequent the Stakis rooms.

Young Hugh's gambling escapades in London were becoming notorious, amounting to nights of madness when he would lose hundreds of thousands on a single outing. Seeing something of the father figure in Reo Stakis, he phoned him at eight-thirty one morning, asking if he would please come round to see him.

Reo turned up at his Buchanan Street office to find him unshaven and full of sleep but simply bursting to show him a cheque.

"I was in London last night and look what I won!" he enthused. The cheque was for £400,000.

"You mean you called me here just to show me this?" asked Stakis. "Well, I'm sorry for you. And you haven't shown me how much you lost in order to win this."

That was the rub. Hugh admired Reo and wanted good opinions in return. But he had come to the wrong person. There was perhaps little point in telling an addict that the casinos are the ones who win in the end. They worked to a profit margin of two and a half per cent and while the gambler's luck may hold for so long, it would not last for ever.

Reo could have told him that the casinos make their money not from the sensible people but from the greediness of the rest. It would have been futile to tell him that the only reasonable way to gamble is to follow what many people do at the racecourses on a social day out. Set aside the amount you are prepared to lose, give up when that point is reached and regard it as the price of your day's entertainment.

But young Hugh Fraser was not Reo's only experience of a gambling disaster. He knew an Italian who had two restaurants in Ayrshire and was a crack hand at poker, winning wherever he went. He said to Reo one day: "You won't be seeing me for a few months, Mr Stakis. I know I'm a good poker player and I'm going to London."

"You're mad," said Stakis. "If I were you I wouldn't play that game again in my life." But once again he was dealing with that frightening addiction, characterised by boasting and self-delusion, which doesn't even have the alcoholic's excuse that the brain was chemically altered by drink.

As warned, he didn't see his Italian friend again for six months. And when he did, he discovered that he had not only lost his money in London but his restaurants in Ayrshire, his home and everything else. Whatever gambles he might take in business, Reo had never been a recreational gambler, professing that he didn't even know one card from another. One of the rules he brought into his casinos, incidentally, was that students were not allowed to participate.

15

LOUGHRAY AND MACDONALD

If John Loughray was the first of the major figures to enter the Stakis orbit, little knowing what the fates would have in store, Donald Macdonald was certainly another who would play a significant part—and end up with an even more surprising denouement.

Macdonald was born in 1947 on Harris, in the Western Isles of Scotland, son of a crofter at Northton, a mere collection of forty houses which sent twenty pupils to the local school. He went from there to Tarbert School but left at the first opportunity and headed for Glasgow, with the intention of joining the police.

Passing the exams but having to wait for six months until he was old enough, he was staying in digs with a man from British Transport Hotels who offered him a job as a junior clerk at the famous Turnberry, just to fill in time until he could join the police. The manager at Turnberry was Jimmy Bannatyne from Arran, who cottoned on to the young lad's talents and said: "You have all the attributes to become a hotel manager."

Donald thought about it, realised he would need two Highers and decided to pursue that course at Langside College, Glasgow. Thus Donald Macdonald took his first step towards the hotel business and forgot all about a career in the police. He served his apprenticeship with British Transport Hotels in Glasgow, at the

Central and St Enoch's but mainly at the North British in George Square, better known today as the Copthorne.

Now aiming at hotel management, he was staying in digs at the home of Mrs Mary Ann Loudon in Maxwell Road, Pollokshields, a lady who came originally from the islands and took that special interest in the boy which may have shaped his whole destiny.

Mrs Loudon lived not far from the home of this Mr Stakis, a gentleman she would meet in the local shop and who impressed her with how polite he was. This was just the kind of man young Donald should be working for, she said. Next, the ever-vigilant Mrs Loudon spotted an advertisement for a job in one of the same Mr Stakis's establishments, Dunblane Hydro—and told him to apply.

Donald took her advice and was called for interview with John Loughray, who was manager of Dunblane at the time. He always remembered turning up for his interview and being asked by Loughray if he wanted a bacon roll. They devoured two each and by the time they were down, the manager had learned enough to offer him the post of junior assistant manager at the prestigious Dunblane Hydro.

It was a tremendous opportunity but, incredibly, when he returned to the North British in Glasgow he allowed himself to be talked out of it by the manager, who told him Reo Stakis was a crazy guy who worked fifteen hours a day and would expect him to work eighteen.

Mrs Loudon was deeply upset that he was turning down the chance to join her Mr Stakis and Donald himself was beginning to feel miserable about his decision. He consulted a young colleague at British Transport Hotels, Ken McCulloch, a prominent name for the future as the one who would bring us restaurants like One Devonshire Gardens and a chain of Malmaisons all over the country.

McCulloch had worked at Stakis and assured him it was a

splendid place to be. That did it. Donald swallowed his pride and phoned John Loughray, confessing that he was the chap who had turned down his offer and was now regretting it. The Dunblane boss said that job was now filled but he was prepared to give him another chance.

That was how Donald Macdonald became senior assistant manager of the Burnbrae Hotel in Bearsden when he was still only twenty-two. He was a quietly intelligent lad, not untypical of the island breed, and soon came to realise the credibility which John Loughray brought to the company.

At that stage in the late 1960s the Stakis empire was still of fairly modest proportions, with some steakhouses and casinos and hotels with names like the Watermill at Paisley, the Redhurst at Giffnock, the Burnside at Rutherglen and Tinto Firs at Kilmarnock Road, Glasgow.

Reo Stakis was a frequent visitor at the Burnbrae where he worked but the quiet-spoken islander did not exactly attract his attention. In fact for the first few months they didn't even speak. The Burnbrae, which was one of the best eating-houses in the west of Scotland, had also become well-known for its folk nights and concerts.

One evening the doorman came to say there was a young man refusing to pay for entry to one of those events—and insisting he was a nephew of Mr Stakis. Macdonald ordered the doorman to put him out but the young man insisted: "My uncle is Reo Stakis."

Macdonald told him: "I don't care who your uncle is."

So he left shouting: "My uncle will sack you!"

Next time Reo Stakis appeared at the Burnbrae he said: "By the way, these functions you run in the evening . . . does everyone pay to get in?"

Yes, they paid. No more was said but the boss looked thoughtful and Macdonald knew what was behind the question. The young man had indeed been a nephew of Reo Stakis, the son of

Harry Nicholas, who owned the Glynhill Hotel at Renfrew. From that day onwards Stakis had a good rapport with Macdonald, knowing that he had done his job, no matter who was involved.

Rather later than might have been, he did move to Dunblane Hydro, at the suggestion of the manager, and was in charge of a function one evening when Mr Stakis arrived. The head of Customs and Excise, who were holding the dinner, began to sing Macdonald's praises to his boss, who was duly appreciative.

At the end of the evening Mr Stakis told him he had been thinking of offering him the manager's job but now he was sure of it. At the age of twenty-four, Macdonald thought his big moment had arrived; but he was soon brought back to earth with a phone-call from John Loughray to say that offer should not have been made. It was not in the best interests of developing his skills and instead he had another job in mind.

"I want you to open a new hotel—the Gantock at Gourock," he consoled. Disappointed about Dunblane, Macdonald wasn't at all sure that he was ready for guiding a completely new venture. Yet he tackled it successfully and laid much store on two key people, Gerry Smith, his number two, and restaurant manager Paco del Gado. The fates must have been at work again because that triumvirate was to come together in another incarnation.

Within two years of Macdonald leaving the Hydro, three managers had failed and each time he went back to John Loughray to ask for the job, hoping to convince him he would have been the right man all along. But Loughray stood firm and said finally: "If you come back once again, I'll fire you!"

In the event, that privilege would not be given to Loughray, who had a high regard for Macdonald. Meanwhile the young man continued his way up the ladder, taking over the Normandy Hotel at Renfrew and becoming an area manager, while all the time talking himself down and saying he was only being promoted because they couldn't find anyone else.

He must have known that that was no more than the pessimism of the misty isles and that he would have a much more significant part to play in the future of Stakis. Just what that part might be—and where his own business future might lie—belonged to another day.

16

LEADING HIS PEOPLE

Having established himself on the Scottish business scene at the end of the Second World War, Reo Stakis realised that the people of Greek origin living here, and seeking to maintain a connection with their own Orthodox Church, had nowhere to worship except in buildings they borrowed from other denominations.

Having clearly emerged as the natural leader of his people in Scotland, he knew there were responsibilities now falling upon his shoulders which he was happy to bear. After all, he was a deeply religious man and life was not all about business.

It was incumbent on him now to lead; so he set about giving his people in Scotland their own place of worship, first buying a smaller building in Grafton Street, Glasgow, before replacing it with the huge edifice of St Luke's Church in Dundonald Street, just off Great Western Road, not far from the Grosvenor Hotel.

Formerly the property of the Episcopal Church of Scotland, this magnificent building was bought by Mr Stakis in 1953 and turned into a religious, cultural and educational centre, with its own priest and a willing band of schoolteachers who give weekend lessons to the youngsters on their own language and background, ethnic dancing and cultural skills. The Stakis children studied Higher Greek at the school and were fully conversant in their parents' tongue which was, in any case, the daily currency of their domestic life.

Reo plays down his part in financing the church, but his contribution over the years runs into hundreds of thousands nevertheless, right up to the 1990s when he was behind an £800,000 refurbishment, with half as much again to come. He was also responsible for much of the student sponsorship from Greece and Cyprus.

In May 1970, the arrival of Nikolaos VI, the Pope and Patriarch of Alexandria and All Africa, turned out to be an event of the highest significance for the Greek community in Scotland. The Patriarch had come to address the General Assembly of the Church of Scotland in Edinburgh, on a day of some disruption which involved the wife of Pastor Jack Glass, a prominent anti-popery figure, himself much given to public protest.

On a happier note, the Patriarch bestowed the Grand Order of St Mark on Reo Stakis for his services to the church and the community. The visit was complete when the Archbishop in London announced that the status of St Luke's Church in Glasgow was being raised to that of a cathedral and would now be known as the Cathedral of St Luke in Scotland.

At a dinner in the Redhurst Hotel that evening, Mr Stakis welcomed an array of dignitaries and said it was an historic day for Glasgow and indeed for Scotland. The Patriarch could now go back and report that the Greek Orthodox community in Scotland was accepted by the other churches and that it was serving the society in which it lived.

If Reo Stakis had become the natural leader and prime benefactor of his people in Scotland, it was also known that his benevolence had stretched to London, where he financed the building of the Chapel of the Archdiocese and later paid for its restoration.

The formal organisation of the Greek Orthodox Church in Britain had preceded his own arrival by only a few years. It was in 1922 that the first Archbishop was installed in London and Reo

Stakis was to befriend all five incumbents who have spanned the 20th century.

His leadership of the community in Scotland—he has been Honorary Commissioner for The Republic of Cyprus at Glasgow since the 1960s—is widely regarded as one of the most significant factors in the story of Greek Orthodoxy in Britain. But having been brought up in its traditions, he felt he was doing no more than his duty to a religion which lays great stress on the need to pass them on to succeeding generations.

It is a Christian Church with a form of service which would not be too far out of reach for other worshippers in Britain. You would hear of the Lord telling his followers: "Seek first of all the Kingdom of God"—and everything else would fall into place.

The Greeks are immensely proud of their ancient language, with texts of sheer beauty and subtlety. They also pride themselves in the fact that the New Testament was originally written in their Greek language and that extended to some books of the Old Testament too.

They will tell you of famous writers and poets they have produced in the 20th century who have used the same Greek as was spoken at the time of the Gospels.

But, as in our western religions, they acknowledge that the younger generations are not so much in tune with archaic forms of speech and, just as there are modern versions of the Bible in the United Kingdom, so have there been less formal translations of the Divine Liturgy for Greeks, as well as translations into English.

As in Britain, there has been much regret expressed, even from within the translation committee, that the changes have taken some of the beauty out of the language. Acknowledging that change would inevitably come, they rather wished it had not happened in their own lifetime.

A Greek community in Britain numbering around 250,000 includes, at any one time, around 30,000 students at British universities, nearly 3000 of them in Scotland. The vast majority of Greeks live in the London area, at first involved in the catering and dressmaking industries but spreading out in more recent times to accountancy, law and many other professions.

In the latter part of the century, their spiritual leader has been Archbishop Gregorios, a Greek Cypriot who was born in Famagusta in 1928, the youngest of nine children whose father died early, leaving their mother with the impossible task of providing a higher education.

The future Archbishop took various jobs in the village, including that of shoemaker, about which he can joke that he was dealing more with soles than souls. But his thirst for knowledge eventually took him on to a secondary education at the Pan-Cyprian Gymnasium in Nicosia and then to the University of Athens, where he studied theology.

His ordination was conducted by Archbishop Makarios and the young priest set out for Britain in 1959, serving at Camden Town, London. With further study at Cambridge, he progressed up the hierarchy until he became Archbishop in 1988, responsible for Ireland and Malta as well as the United Kingdom.

Curiously, his quarter-million flock in this country includes not only Greeks but people from the former Soviet Union, Poland, Latvia, Romania and Bulgaria, as well as Arabs, and even takes in an increasing number of Britons who have turned to the tradition of Orthodoxy. There was no Reformation in the religion but Orthodox Christians were under the yoke of the Ottoman Empire for hundreds of years. Cyprus was taken by the British in 1878 but agitated for the independence which was gained in 1960, after the guerrilla warfare of the 1950s.

Britain retained sovereignty of two areas but Cyprus has remained a divided island, fought over by the majority Greek community and the much smaller Turkish one. After the Turkish invasion of 1974, Greeks fled to safer havens and Archbishop

Gregorios was among those who were unable to return to their native Famagusta.

As the religious leader in Britain, he has paid regular visits to Scotland, where his people worship in Edinburgh, Aberdeen, Dundee, St Andrews and Stirling as well as Glasgow. When they first met, he was intrigued to discover the background of Reo Stakis, since he knew about his native village of Kato-Drys before he had heard of the man himself.

By coincidence, his sister had worked at the gathering of the carob crop in the village and had come home with glowing tales of the generosity of the people and the quality of their houses, at least compared to those in her own village.

But the Archbishop was not long in Britain before he realised the significance of Reo Stakis in relation to his own predecessors, dating back to the 1920s when he had arrived with that caseful of his mother's lace. As a young priest in Britain, Gregorios would learn that Mr Stakis was a welcome visitor at the home of the Archbishop and when he himself was ordained as a bishop in 1970, Reo attended the ceremony in London.

The Archbishop paid him this tribute: "As a people, we admire and respect Reo Stakis not only for his business achievements but for his humility, his kindness and generosity, his understanding and faith in God. When I first came to Glasgow I was impressed by how well-known and highly regarded he was by his employees.

"When discussing anything with him, you realised that he was listening all the time and, when he did speak, it was sensible things he had to say. Some people have much education and high positions in life but they lack the essential humanity, integrity and humble faith of the man in the street. Reo Stakis has a vast knowledge of religion and a rare understanding of faith."

17

MAKARIOS: MAN OF DESTINY

Those in search of omens could find one to suggest that Reo Stakis might have expected some link with church and state in his native Cyprus. For just as he was seeing the first light of day in his village of Kato-Drys, towards the eastern side of the island, in 1913, another baby was born towards the western end, near the town of Paphos, now well-known to British holidaymakers.

His name was Mihail Christodoulou Mouskos, destined to become perhaps the most famous Cypriot of all—and one of the most publicised political leaders of the 20th century—under his better-known name of Archbishop Makarios.

The mixing of religion and politics was a Byzantine tradition which virtually ended with Makarios who, as so often in the history of the British Empire, was the thorn in the flesh of the colonial power who ended up as the leader of his people. While a priest and later Archbishop of the Greek Orthodox Church during the 1950s, he came under well-founded suspicion of being a collaborator with the anti-British guerrilla forces known as the EOKA.

On an island ripped apart by conflict between Greek and Turkish communities, the balance was sought by the Governor-General of the day, distinguished wartime leader Field Marshal Sir John Harding. Makarios, who had become head of the Greek-Cypriot community, was finally deported to his exile in the Seychelles, sparking riots and threats of a massive bombing campaign by EOKA forces.

Sir John Harding claimed he had been removed as "a major obstacle to a return to peaceful conditions" and that the Archbishop had actively fostered terrorism. He had inspired Colonel Grivas, a former Greek army officer, to form EOKA, which had conducted its campaign in Cyprus from 1953. Many a British soldier of those days has memories of fighting EOKA in the Troodos Mountains, a picturesque setting which today presents an impressive shrine to the same Archbishop Makarios.

His restoration as a respectable figure came about with the 1959 agreement which gave the island its independence, Makarios returning as head of state, the first President of the Republic of Cyprus. Only then could he take on the full responsibilities of his country, which of course included the ongoing difficulties between Greeks and Turks.

He was also under fire from his own bishops for his dual role in politics and religion. Indeed there was a coup, inspired by the reigning military junta on mainland Greece, which briefly removed him from power in 1974 but he was back in time for his closing years. He died in 1977, aged sixty-four, a much-loved leader of his people, who then separated the roles of archbishop and head-of-state.

Naturally, all of this was followed with deep interest and not a little mixed feeling by Makarios's fellow-countryman and precise contemporary in Scotland. Reo Stakis had come to know him at an early stage, assessing the power and determination of the man while acknowledging that he extended all the way to stubbornness.

His first encounter with Makarios dated back to the days of his motorbike and sidecar, when he was paying a visit back home to Cyprus from his peripatetic existence in Britain. His maternal grandfather, the priest, was still alive and wished to attend an ordination ceremony for this young man called Makarios, who had entered the priesthood of the Greek Orthodox Church.

So Reo offered to take the old man to Paphos, home of Makarios where the ceremony was being held, and off they set, grandson in the driving seat with the priestly grandpa in the sidecar, his robes of office blowing in the wind.

"He looked like a ghost," Reo recalled, "and as we passed through villages on the way, the people were making the sign of the Cross."

But that was just the start of his contact with the figure who would one day become his people's man of destiny. Real acquaintance came through his friendship with George Charalambous, to whose child Reo Stakis was godfather. George was adviser to the Abbot of Kikkos and wanted Reo to meet Makarios, who had attended the monastery there during his youth.

Reo was basically a non-political animal but the Archbishop was keen to talk to people, to listen and to absorb information. Being based in Britain, his new-found acquaintance would be an interesting contact. From Reo's point of view, apart from enjoying the conversation and close study of an historic figure, there was the commercial interest of knowing that the Orthodox Church owned a lot of land.

His business mind was never too far from thoughts of development and, yes, despite his well-established life in the United Kingdom, he would not be averse to building a hotel or two on his native island. Where better to serve the tourist trade?

Reo came round to asking Makarios if he would sell him some church land and there was an agreement that he would. He had spotted an idyllic location for a hotel, where four bays came together, with vines in the background and fir trees rising beyond that.

He reckoned it was the most perfect site you could wish to find and went home to discuss it with his brewery contacts at Scottish and Newcastle, who had become a vital part of Stakis financing. They too were interested and accompanied him to Cyprus, where they decided to invest if possible.

Reo asked Makarios if Cyprus would put something towards the project but all he would offer was £100,000. They shelved it for the time being but the next thing they heard was that an old friend of Stakis, the equally colourful Charles Forte, was planning a development there—and that Makarios had put up at least £1 million of it!

Reo confronted the President: "Why did you do that for Forte and you couldn't do it for us?" Makarios's reply was to the effect that he didn't know about conducting such deals until he spoke to Stakis. Now he knew to offer a better deal to the developer! It seemed like the height of ingratitude that he didn't afford his own friend and compatriot the benefit of the advice he had given. It was also indicative of a rather dubious streak in the man's nature.

The contact with Makarios was maintained, however, and Reo Stakis became a familiar visitor both at his home at Strovolos and at the Presidential Palace in Nicosia. He judged the Archbishop to be a good businessman, clever and astute, and the two of them would sit deep in discussion till the early hours of the morning. Makarios knew he was listening to the voice of a successful property man and did not miss the chance to pick his brains.

For all the friendship which developed between the two men— and for all the advice imparted—there was always a sense that Makarios would use you for his own particular purpose. Reo remembered him as a fiercely strong-willed man; whatever he said, he insisted on being carried through. It was largely because of the troubles between Greeks and Turks, which continued to erupt, that the land deal he promised never did materialise.

But on some of those visits to Makarios he would take Annitsa and the children and on such occasions the President would show another side of his nature, spending endless time with the young-sters, telling them fascinating stories from his early days near Paphos and how he finally reached power in the palace. The Stakis children sat riveted by the historic tales they were hearing from their own ethnic background.

But just as Reo Stakis became the friend of the Archbishop, so in his later life did he gain the friendship of Lord Harding, the Governor-General who had to cope with the machinations of Makarios and his cohorts during the troubles of the 1950s.

A Somerset man, Harding rose to be Chief-of-Staff of the Allied army in Italy in 1944, a much-respected soldier who faced one of his stiffest tasks when he was appointed to the Cyprus post in 1955. His brief was to reorganise the security forces and seek to counter the terrorism of the time. He certainly established order through martial law and banished Makarios, though he did not succeed in bringing about a political settlement.

That came soon afterwards however and in retrospect he would discuss those days with Reo Stakis, who had gained a deep regard for the British soldier. He found Harding to be a straight and honest man who revealed that, while he respected Makarios, he found him to be possessed of a thoroughly obstinate and unpro-ductive streak.

Even when he was assuring him that he was working earnestly towards peace in Cyprus, Makarios would leave no scope for manoeuvre, always pulling in the rope to his own advantage. The assurance that the colonies were going to be liberated and his pleas for patience brought no response whatever.

Reo Stakis could naturally see both sides of the story but had no problem of divided loyalties. He was pro-British all the way and knew better than most the difficulty of the situation, not unlike that of Northern Ireland. It just continued to sadden him that such bitterness could persist when his own recollection of early days in Kato-Drys was of two sides getting on well together. His mother's helpers in creating her lace were mainly Turks and at the personal level there was never a problem.

So Reo Stakis had a highly-privileged view of those two key men in the history of Cyprus, later renewing contact with Makarios in London, when he was the guest of their mutual friend, Charles Forte, the man he had favoured with that Cyprus deal of many years before.

He could only reflect on his homeland and its troubles and know that his most ardent prayers were for some kind of reconciliation. He had always dreamed that his beautiful island, with its privileged location and sunny people, would one day become known as the Pearl of the Mediterranean.

18

A LESSON IN BETTING

Back in Scotland, the grind of progress was such that the opening of yet another Stakis establishment became a regular event, as the man himself grew in business stature and reputation, not unlike the style of Charles Forte, if on a more modest scale.

In later years he could sit back in his chair and break into a smile over some of the deals he managed to strike in the 1960s. In one day, for example, he bought three hotels, the Station and Golden Lion in Stirling and the Ancaster in the small town of Callander. Yet before that week was out he had sold the Golden Lion and the Ancaster at a profit which not only left him with the Station Hotel for nothing but with surplus cash as well.

The innocent bystander might wonder why the people who bought those two hotels had not seen the same opportunity earlier in the week, when they could obviously have landed them for much less. It is the talent of people like Reo Stakis that they spot these opportunities and foresee the deals which can be achieved. History also shows that incomers to a country tend to take chances which locals have either failed to see or didn't want to risk. It is the story of many a Jew or Pakistani who has made a fortune in another country.

Reo Stakis was often asked why he had sold the Golden Lion and the Ancaster when they were regarded as profitable. His simple answer was that the Station Hotel was making three times as much as the other two put together. But there was slightly more to it than that. Quite clearly, by the simplest possible means, the deal had provided the finance to acquire a hotel without borrowing a penny. It was wheeler-dealing at its most successful.

At that stage, he claimed, it was not so easy to raise money as it has been in more recent times; so it was necessary to bring off an occasional coup like that.

For those who believed that the best opportunities in business lay in the past, Reo Stakis had a very different story. In the latter part of the century he was telling budding businessmen: "The opportunities now are better than ever before. If you are willing to work and have the initiative, money is easier to come by. But you must know your business. If you don't know it, don't go for it. If you do know it, then you must be ready to take your chances.

"The most difficult part used to be making your first £100,000. Now you can call that your first million. After that, people begin to come to you. You will have proved yourself to be a worthwhile businessman and they will recognise that. Having started from nothing, you have come this far. That impresses people.

"And no matter how good you are, you must develop the judgement to know how to buy when prices are low and sell when they are high. It's common sense. Even outwith catering, which was my business, I was constantly buying and selling, hopefully at the right time and price.

"We bought the Barracuda Casino in Baker Street, London, for £11 million and were happy with it. But when we were offered £27 million, we sold it. The same would happen with the St Ermin's Hotel in London if the price was right. [That came to pass in 1998, though the company retained the management of it.] But even when you sell, I have found it is always good to leave something for the next person. If you simply try to squeeze everything for yourself, you will be the loser at the end of the day."

The purchase of the St Ermin's had been a landmark in the life of Mr Stakis. He had long harboured an ambition to move into the hotel market in London, the city he had first glimpsed that bleak day of 1928 when the thief ran off with his case of lace. He had been looking around Earls Court for some time but the capital city was proving an expensive hunting ground.

In January 1983, however, he launched a rights issue to raise £7.7 million. With that sum, a bid was made for the St Ermin's, a popular hotel neatly tucked into a cul-de-sac beside New Scotland Yard and within easy walking distance of the Houses of Parliament. At £6.5 million, a deal was clinched with the owners, Grand Metropolitan, representing the biggest buy in the history of the company.

The four-star St Ermin's, with its 290 bedrooms and chintzy look, became the flagship. It was next door to the famous registry office of Caxton Hall and that property, too, was secured when the function of civil wedding ceremonies was discontinued. In a more recent development, planning permission was sought for partly restoring the registry purpose.

By the spring of 1998, however, the company had sold the leasehold of the St Ermin's to an American real estate firm, Strategic Hotel Capital Incorporated (SHCI) for £47.75 million. Stakis retained the contract for managing the hotel for at least thirty years, a modern method of operation which had the advantage of saving capital.

In his advice to young businessmen, Reo Stakis would illustrate his stories to show that he was not always the winner, emphasising the lesson about sticking to what you know. He once succumbed to an overture from two young men from the Robert Burns village of Alloway in Ayrshire who had a bright idea.

Over coffee at the Normandy Hotel, he heard from Ken McKeown and Peter Denman of their ambition to make aluminium for the vehicle and construction industries. It sounded like a progressive idea and he was encouraged to invest £300,000 in the Olympic Aluminium Company at Irvine, even though he knew nothing about the industry. On that occasion his instincts were wrong and when that business went down the drain he lost a lot of money. This was a personal venture, outwith the Stakis organisation, but the pain was no less acute!

He could tell of another which came unstuck. Casinos may have been good for the organisation but the betting-shop business was not. Stakis had taken over the bookmaking empire built up by a well-known Glasgow figure, Tony Queen, close friend of Jock Stein and the man who was in the car with the Celtic boss when they were involved in a horrendous crash from which Stein never fully recovered.

The company would now be called Queen Bookmakers and another popular Glasgow figure was engaged to run it. John Macfarlane, formerly the boss of William Hill in Scotland and Northern Ireland, introduced what he called the Champion Fixed Odds, which was run from an office in New City Road.

It was based on five results but, with Clydebank on a glorious run, the punters were adding Rangers, Celtic and Manchester United and needed just one more win to crack it.

Other bookmakers had also brought their businesses to the Stakis doorstep but soon there was a feeling that this was not for them. Whereas the Stakis people knew something about gaming in general, they discovered that, while you don't lose money in casinos, you can very easily lose it in the betting shop. So they cut their losses and ran.

But there was always another adventure round the corner. The Ca'dora had long been a famous Glasgow institution at the corner of Union Street and Gordon Street, the type of complex which was neither hotel nor conventional restaurant but a convenient venue for wedding receptions and similar functions. It also had baths; indeed, young Reo Stakis selling lace in the 1930s would drop into the Ca'dora for his ablutions as well as his meal. There was even a barber's shop where he would sit down for a trim and a chat with his favourite barber, the young Alex Frutin, before he became well-known in Glasgow's theatrical circles.

But that kind of place went out of fashion and the splendid building was lying empty when Reo Stakis took it over on a lease from the owners, the City Bakeries. He turned it into the Tropicana Restaurant, with a cabaret room in the class of the Chevalier, bringing north top artistes of the Sixties from Matt Monro, Roy Castle and Millicent Martin to Ronnie Hilton, Rolf Harris, Lita Rosa and Jackie Trent.

Miss Trent was soon to marry Tony Hatch, then the recording boss of Pye, and together they would write many hit-tunes of the day, from "Don't Sleep in the Subway" to the theme music for the television series *Neighbours*, which survived throughout the rest of the century.

Reo Stakis had opened the Pandora in Victoria Road as well as the huge Dalriada on Edinburgh Road, Glasgow, which could boast a 45-foot-long bar, with a dozen beer pumps and parking for a hundred cars, all spectacular features at the time.

The man's persuasive powers could be gauged from his experience at the Invercarse Hotel on Perth Road, Dundee. Dropping in to see the French lady who ran it, he asked if she might be interested in selling. She politely offered him a coffee but the answer to his question was a resounding "No!" By the time he finished his coffee he had bought the Invercarse! It is a story which supports the theory that everything has its price, so hotly denied in some quarters. He merely shrugs and mentions a sum which must have sounded like a lot of money at the time. People have a habit of being responsive to arguments like that.

Soon there was hardly a small town in Scotland which didn't

have a Stakis pub or hotel or restaurant, whether it was the Harness in Edinburgh's Fountainbridge, the Granary in Helensburgh, the Plough in Ayr, the Tower in East Kilbride or the City Mills in Perth. In that last development, he converted an old mill in the town centre in 1970 and gained an award for having retained the traditional features, like the mill-wheel and the kingpin which secured the ceiling.

In 1965 he took over Oughton's of Dumfries, which had served the town as a first-class restaurant for more than fifty years. The former entrance and bakery shop were transformed into the Beachcomber Bar and lounge, with an attractive dining-room upstairs and a steakhouse above that.

Stakis had bought Oughton's from the Western SMT and customers of the old premises were pleasantly surprised to step through the doorway and behold the new decor. Alterations had cost £50,000 and the refurbishment, making room for 200 people, was fairly typical of the fresh excitement which Stakis was bringing to the ambience of eating-houses in Scotland.

Back in Glasgow, he had opened everything from the Waterloo inn and pub in Waterloo Street and the Quo Vadis in Paisley Road West to the Doune Castle in Kilmarnock Road and the improbably-named Hecla and Butty in Drumchapel. He had also acquired another famous name in the city's catering history, the Marlborough at Shawlands, which came into the same category as the Ca'dora, complete with beautiful chandeliers and a popular venue for wedding and other receptions.

19

THE STAKIS STEAKHOUSE

In creating the concept of the steakhouse, nothing had been more significant than the Georgic, arising out of the redevelopment of Glasgow in the 1960s, when there was a general sweeping away of the old tenements, sometimes to be replaced by the bleak architecture of that decade.

This was typified by some of the high-rise blocks of flats in the Gorbals and elsewhere—which involved even a famous Scottish architect, Sir Basil Spence, counted among the great names of world architecture, not least for his adventurous design of the new Coventry Cathedral which would arise from the ashes of the German blitz during the Second World War. As far as his work in Glasgow was concerned, there was a general view that, instead of being awarded a knighthood, Sir Basil should have been charged with offending the human eye.

Part of that general demolition of old Glasgow was the razing of shops along the city's George Street from George Square towards High Street. The old Royal College of Science and Technology was just about the only building to survive but now that it was aspiring to the status of a university there was a search for more accommodation. As it happened, a multi-storey office-block had just replaced some of those old shops on the north side of George Street but the venture was meeting with a decided lack of enthusiasm from potential occupants.

Someone had the bright idea of adapting this high-rise white elephant for the needs of what was now to be Strathclyde University and that is where that noble institution is based today.

On the ground level of George Street, however, that tower-block had been laid out for retail shopping and one of its first occupants was Reo Stakis, pursuing his dream of a chain of steakhouses. It was a good site, well placed not only for the university and surrounding business community but for Lord Beaverbrook's Scottish Daily Express in Albion Street, just round the corner, where no fewer than 2000 people were employed in Scotland's biggest newspaper operation.

Indeed it was one of the Express's finest talents, Don Whyte (his father was Ian Whyte, founder-conductor of the BBC Scottish Symphony Orchestra) who went across to write about the new arrival on the Express doorstep. Don Whyte's description serves as good evidence of what Reo Stakis was trying to achieve at a time when eating habits were much less sophisticated than he would make them in the years ahead.

"New buildings have a way of brooding like characterless cliffs over our accustomed landscape. It takes the persuasion of artists to mellow modernity," wrote Don. "It took a deal of artistry to create the Georgic and give it an old-world atmosphere in the midst of cold steel and reinforced concrete.

"Newest in the Reo Stakis line of steakhouses, the Georgic does not bludgeon you with chromium and stuck-on washable surfaces. It lets good work speak for itself. Tables are of oak; and so are the monks' bench seats with their tapestry upholstery. Plastic and paint-work are minimal.

"Your generous steak arrives on an oval platter (the better to accommodate its dimensions) and is placed on a copper table-mat. You eat and drink and pause to appraise your surroundings. You look up to an airy ceiling of old English wattles above which is a super ventilation system. It makes you feel like a well-fed dryad.

"The Georgic is full of effective touches. The bottoms of wine bottles have been used to panel the bar front, illuminated from the inside. There are Tyrolean hanging lamps and Bavarian lanterns. The bar gantry is Gothic in style and there are old shutter windows, subtly lit. Templetons, the carpet experts, have spread a rich pile with black motif across the floor while rough-cast pillars make a cool framework for the scene.

"For twelve shillings you can have a grilled fillet steak with French fried potatoes, mushroom, tomatoes, roll and butter, sweet or biscuits and cheese. There is an ample wine cellar and one speciality of the house is sherry drawn from the cask."

Thus Don Whyte, himself a wonderful painter as well as master wordsmith, was giving a contemporary, artistic view of the type of steakhouse which was still a novelty in Scotland in the mid-1960s. Though Don was treating himself to a twelve-shilling meal with fillet steak, it was possible to enjoy a full dinner for less than half that price. (About 27 pence today!)

In the ups-and-downs of trying to extend his empire, Stakis was granted the licence for a new £120,000 hotel at Thornliebank, on the south side of Glasgow, but refused the licence for a sixteen-bedroom, £100,000 hotel at Burnside, Rutherglen. Within weeks, however, the appeal court reversed the Thornliebank decision and he had to start all over again. A few months later and the perseverance paid off. The authority granted both licences and that was how the Avion at Thornliebank and the Burnside Hotel came into being. To complete the hat-trick, he was granted a public-house licence for the Mushroom Restaurant at East Kilbride.

In selling a considerable slice of his empire to Scottish and Newcastle in 1965, Reo not only surprised the business world but proved that nothing was ever static at Stakis. That sale included three popular wining-and-dining spots in Glasgow, the Gondola in Hope Street, the Sans Souci in Glassford Street and the famous old Ca'dora in Union Street, where only two weeks earlier he had entertained Princess Alexandra and Mr Angus Ogilvy after a Stars for Spastics charity night at the Metropole.

But there was always method in the madness. He explained that the money realised from the sale would go to the financing of new projects. "I'm always looking for new sites and have sixteen projects in hand," he explained. His Ivy Restaurant had become the Alfa and he had gained the franchise for the Kelvin Hall in Glasgow, which was the principal venue in those days for everything from the Scottish Motor Show and carnivals to world championship boxing matches when Scotland was nurturing young talents like Jim Watt.

With hotels being opened every few months, Stakis picked up one of his rarest bargains when the Halfway House, on the Glasgow-Ayr road near Hansel Village, was given to him for a token £1000 by Scottish and Newcastle, who recognised that it was in a run-down state and didn't look a good prospect in any case.

So the hurly-burly of business continued, a daily adventure which stirred the adrenaline of men like Reo Stakis. But he was the first to acknowledge that it could not be achieved on his own. Apart from his in-house lieutenants like John Loughray and Donald Macdonald, there were people on the outside who were vital to his enterprise and who built whole careers and business structures largely on the back of a man like Stakis.

Above: Reo with his father in Cyprus

Left: His mother, Katerina. Reo came to Britain in 1928 to sell the lace she made

Reo and Annitsa on their wedding day, 1946

With his sons Andros and Evros as teenagers

The Stakis daughters at Ridi's wedding. From left: Stassia, Ridi, Niki, Rena

Reo engaged in his main relaxation—grouse shooting—at Crawfordjohn on 12th August, 1963

Reo had four key executives in the heyday of the Stakis organisation.
Clockwise from top left:
Donald Macdonald, Frank O'Callaghan, Stuart Jenkins, John Loughray

Above: David Michels, chief executive in the 1990s

Above: Andros Stakis, Sir Reo's son and heir

Below: An informal boardroom study of the 1990s. Sir Reo (second left) is with Ian Bankier, Ian Payne, Neil Chisman, Richard Cole-Hamilton, David Michels, Anthony Harris, Robert Smith (chairman). Sir Charles Fraser is in the foreground

Above: Sir Charles Fraser, leading Edinburgh lawyer.
He masterminded vital changes at Stakis

Opposite: Proud day at the Palace. Sir Reo with Lady Stakis,
after receiving his knighthood on 2nd November, 1988

Below: Sir Lewis Robertson, brought in as the "company doctor"

Right: The plush Riverboat Casino on Glasgow's Broomielaw—landmark on the city's waterfront

Below: In picturesque setting, the Dunblane Hydro became a splendid addition to the Stakis empire in 1962

Left: The gracious foyer of the London St Ermin's hotel, which became the flagship of the Stakis organisation

Below: The magnificent Regency-style Grosvenor Hotel, one of Glasgow's most impressive façades

The Grosvenor in less happy times: Reo surveys the fire damage in 1978.
The hotel was subsequently restored to its full splendour

In Cyprus with the island's first president, Archbishop Makarios.
Members of the family are in the background

Above: Accompanied by Reo Stakis and Scots comedian Jack Radcliffe, popular Latin American bandleader Edmundo Ros performs the opening of the Copacabana

Below: Charity nights bring Reo into contact with showbusiness personalities, like Moira Anderson and Johnny Beattie

Above: Happy times with Jimmy Logan, a friend of Reo

Below: More glittering showbiz nights with familiar faces,
including Frankie Howerd and Eric Sykes

Above: With his native village of Kato-Drys in the background,
Sir Reo revisits Cyprus in 1998

Below: An audience with the president of Cyprus in 1998.
Glafcos Clerides served as an RAF pilot during the Second World War

20

NO MIRRORS PLEASE!

Just as Reo Stakis looked for regular guidance from Hugh McCalman as lawyer and friend, so did he depend hugely on the man whose architect's practice would create and convert buildings wherever the Stakis logo appeared.

Born in 1928, Tom Miller had grown up at Muirend on the south side of Glasgow, qualified as an architect and set up his own small practice in Lynedoch Crescent. With the advantage of a strong and distinctive personality, he was destined to become the kind of entrepreneurial architect who would appeal to a man like Reo Stakis. That is exactly what happened.

Miller was specialising in small houses and pubs when he came to the notice of the man whose catering business was taking off in a big way from the advent of the Sixties. Tom Miller began to flourish in tandem, aided by two partners who would continue the association after his premature death.

Stuart Wallace remembers how it all developed, having grown up in Clarkston, not far from Miller's home, in the thirties and forties, before qualifying as an architect in 1954, working for Boswell, Mitchell and Johnston and undertaking his National Service in 1955-57. Unsettled after the military, he happened to meet in with Tom, who had qualified two years ahead of him, was establishing himself on the Glasgow scene—and was offering him a job, with the promise of a partnership to follow a year later.

Having come from the sophistication of Boswell, Mitchell and Johnston, Stuart Wallace found himself entering a very different environment on the day he turned up to start work at Lynedoch Crescent. For one thing, Tom Miller was not in the office. He may have gone off for a few days but he had not forgotten to leave instructions as to how his new colleague could occupy himself. Whereas the young architect might have been asked to design a door in his last place of work, the Miller expectation was somewhat higher. "Design a thirty-bedroom hotel!" was the gist of the message.

Stuart gulped in surprise but quietly buckled down to the task. However serious the expectation, when Tom Miller returned to the office he was flabbergasted to find that young Wallace had taken him at his word—and was presenting him with a full set of drawings for a new hotel on the east side of Glasgow!

Needless to say, he was soon to discover that much of the work was coming from this up-and-coming name on the Glasgow scene, Reo Stakis. Not that Mr Stakis was altogether unknown to Stuart Wallace and his friend Bob Burnett. As students in pursuit of a half-crown lunch, they used to frequent the Princes Restaurant in those early days when Mr Stakis was circulating among the tables and personally welcoming his customers.

He would chat in his attractively animated, Cypriot style of English and little would he have guessed that the young men, just another couple of students, would one day play such an important part in creating the distinctive, physical features of what the public came to recognise as a Stakis establishment.

Stuart Wallace and Bob Burnett would later marvel at how their respective careers matched each other step by step. They had walked into Glasgow School of Art together on that first day in 1948; they had worked together at Boswell, Mitchell and Johnston and had gone off to the army together.

When Stuart joined Tom Miller, he was sitting in the office one day when the phone rang. "It's for you," said Tom. The call was from Bob Burnett, who sounded dejected and was asking if Stuart would meet him for lunch.

When he came off the phone, Stuart explained to Tom Miller who he was. "Is he any good?" asked Tom.

"He's very good," said Stuart.

"When you're having lunch, offer him a job here—on the same terms as yourself."

Bob Burnett had been attending interviews and was still downhearted. So Stuart was not only pleased to see him but happy at the prospect of cheering him up. "How would you like to work for us?"

That question not only cheered him up but set Bob on a similar career to that of his friend. He too became a partner within a year and the three men were now in place as the triumvirate which would carry the Miller Partnership to high success.

Tom Miller was a master at making contacts and it was through his concentration on designing public houses that he first came into the orbit of Reo Stakis. Of personable demeanour and always smartly dressed, though rather too portly in build, he exuded confidence and inspired it in other people.

He was doing work for Scottish and Newcastle, William Hill the bookmakers and of course Reo Stakis. Another client was the Sportswork company, based in Royal Crescent, Glasgow, and when they moved out to Bishopbriggs, Tom Miller moved his practice into their former premises.

Because of his contacts, he could switch quite smartly from one sector to another. When the hotels were not so busy, his staff would find themselves working for the Ravenscraig Steelworks at Motherwell.

He was also well acquainted with Matt Taylor, the haulier and vice-chairman of Rangers Football Club, and was asked to tackle the architectural work demanded as a result of the Ibrox Disaster of January 1971. On that tragic day—a forerunner of the Hillsborough Disaster in England—sixty-six people were killed in a crowd collapse at the end of the New Year's Day match between Rangers and Celtic.

Celtic seemed to have won the game by a single goal and the Rangers supporters were already leaving the ground in disappointment when their team scored a dramatic last-minute equaliser. In their sudden delight, there was crush and confusion on a steep stairway leading from the top of the terracing towards the exit. Ironically, the tragedy took place on Stairway No 13.

The ensuing architectural work was just the beginning of Tom Miller's major contracts at Ibrox. Rangers later decided to remodel the stadium, building grandstands on three sides of the ground. Stuart Wallace, who was in charge of that project, was actually more interested in rugby than football and had designed the grandstand for Clarkston Rugby Club, in Tom Miller's native corner of Muirend. After the successful creation of a new-style Ibrox Stadium, he found himself deeply involved in the design of a new-look home for Scottish rugby at Murrayfield.

Tom Miller had an uncanny knack of getting to the heart of a problem. He would tell his people: "It's not the mistakes you make, it's the way you get out of them that matters." The client was everything to him. He lived in some style in Busby, on the southern fringe of Glasgow, and built an extension to his house for the purpose of entertaining his clients. The theory was that the client was the boss, the man who paid your wages.

He would never interrupt Reo Stakis on the phone if he knew he was busy at a board meeting but he did not mind if Reo interrupted him. That was the client's prerogative.

Wallace and Burnett were soon into the swing of working for the hotelier. After Stuart's dramatic initiation into the Miller methods, he was soon involved in one of the best-known Stakis hotels, the Tinto Firs on Kilmarnock Road, Glasgow, though that design was mainly in the hands of Bob Burnett.

They all remembered how they worked on converting that old Naafi building into the Chevalier casino and restaurant at the top of Buchanan Street. It was a new experience for Miller's architects and they were soon to learn from initial mistakes. For example, they had installed some splendid mirrors, forgetting that you cannot have mirrors in a casino! When something like that was discovered, they were up all hours of the night—in the case of the Chevalier engaged in papering over the offending glass.

Stuart Wallace reckoned he learned some valuable lessons by studying the demeanour and attitudes of Reo Stakis. One Sunday morning he dropped his children at Sunday School and proceeded to the site of the Chevalier casino. Too late, he realised that he still had the children's hymn-books in the back of the car. When Mr Stakis arrived from his own church service, Stuart was telling him about the hymn-books.

"Mr Wallace," he said with a quiet smile, "you don't TAKE your children to church. You GO with your children to church."

At cocktail parties, Stuart Wallace knew full well that people would come up to talk with business prospects in mind. He had noticed that wives would be ignored because they had nothing to offer in that respect. His own wife Audrey had met Reo Stakis for the first time at the opening of the Chevalier.

The next occasion was a considerable time later, at the Tinto Firs. Yet when Mr Stakis arrived he went straight across and said: "Hello, Mrs Wallace, how good to see you." The little touches mattered. He remembered people and made them feel the better of his presence. Indeed the courtesy and consideration he showed towards his own wife was extended to ladies in general.

For all the steely qualities required in a successful businessman, there is more of a heart than we sometimes suspect. Reo Stakis had always had an instinct for people and a genuine caring and concern for them. He invited Stuart Wallace to lunch at the Grosvenor one day in 1983, when it transpired that there was something on his mind.

Reo wanted to express apprehension about Tom Miller. "I'm very worried about him," he said. "Is he ill?"

Stuart had not been aware of anything but learned later that one of the partners had noticed tension building up over a particular contract.

Two weeks later, Tom Miller was dead. He had suffered an aneurysm and was gone at the age of fifty-five, causing shock among his large circle of friends. People like Willie Waddell, one-time hard man of Rangers, both as player and manager, were openly in tears at the funeral, such was the impact of the man.

Reo Stakis took over the arrangements for the funeral reception, providing for the mourners at the Redhurst Hotel, appropriately since that had been one of their early partnerships, in which they laid down the pattern for the kind of "roadhouse" hotel which would become popular in that era.

Stuart Wallace, who would take over as head of the firm, had had his own problems shortly before Tom's death, having suffered a heart attack at the age of fifty-two. He was spared a role at the funeral when Bob Burnett ably stepped in to give the eulogy.

By then, the Miller firm had grown to seven partners and was one of the biggest in town. Stuart Wallace felt a certain apprehension about the future, remembering the close connection of Tom and Reo, between whom there was such a bond of mutual trust. But he need not have feared. The loyalty which Stakis showed to people like Tom Miller would be extended to his successors.

For Tom had gone to great lengths to set standards and make sure his clients had everything they required—and then something extra. When a building was completed he wouldn't leave the client to attend to cleaners and decorators. He would see to that himself. There was a subtlety in the relationship in that they would use first names in banter but invariably revert to "Mister Stakis" and "Mister Miller" in all matters of business. It was an etiquette to which they strictly adhered. When the two men dined together Tom would consult the menu and say to the manager: "What do you recommend for slimming?" Picking up on the spirit of banter, the manager would say: "Why don't you try jogging, Sir?"

Stuart Wallace was relieved to find that Mr Stakis stuck with the firm right through. He and Bob Burnett carried on just as they had done in Tom Miller's day and all three could be said to have had a life completely fulfilled in architecture. Ten years after Tom's death, Stuart and Bob, having had such a coincidence of careers, both retired on the same day of 1993, great friends who even extended the parallel to the fact that both families had houses at Lamlash.

21

TO THE STOCK MARKET

Tony Langiano spent his early years as a professional musician, playing banjo and guitar with bands like Jim McHarg in those jazz-revival days of the early Sixties. He was the son of an Italian immigrant who came to Scotland for the traditional purpose of owning a café and decided he could make life easier for his children by shortening the family name.

So his son became Tony Lang, not only a musician but a qualified accountant who joined the Stakis organisation in 1965 as another key player in the team which would see the name expand in the public consciousness. He began as assistant to the chief accountant at a time when the Scottish public was discovering that there was an alternative to the traditional choice of a tea-room or an upmarket restaurant. It was the Stakis steakhouse.

Tony Lang sensed that things were on the move within the company. He took his cue from the accountant, the popular Don Cornock, who had switched from being a professional footballer and was now playing a major part in the development of Stakis. Sadly, Cornock suffered a head injury and was found wandering in Hamilton one day, unaware of where he was. It transpired that he had been the victim of a brain haemorrhage and died as a young man.

Into the 1970s the Stakis organisation had passed its silver jubilee and was reaching a major crossroads. A level of growth had been attained where a decision would have to be taken about going public. For Reo Stakis it was the dilemma of many an entrepreneur who builds his own business from scratch, only to face the prospect that it will drift out of his immediate control. There will be shareholders and analysts and City people poking their noses into what was once your own private business, preventing you from being master of your own destiny.

By his own steely efforts, he had led an organisation which began to show real growth around 1960 and within a dozen years had reached the proportion of sixty-six establishments, from hotels and steakhouses to pubs, restaurants and casinos.

In 1972, however, Reo Stakis faced the fact that the company which bore his name must now be floated on the Stock Exchange, though he made no pretence that he was leaping for joy at the thought of it.

Until now, growth had been financed by three main methods: through property deals; by ploughing back profits; and by substantial borrowing from the Scottish and Newcastle brewers who stocked all Stakis bars. By 1977, however, the company would have to begin repaying around £2 million to Scottish and Newcastle—and there were plans to borrow as much again before April 1975.

For all the natural inclination to keep hold of the baby, business sense would dictate that proper development needed broader access to public money. The new issue would ease the cash flow. At that point, Tony Lang was asked to take over as company secretary.

In fact there had been an attempt to go public a year earlier but that proved to be a false start. Insufficient information was being provided to the bankers to justify the price of the shares, which as some insiders knew was a more polite way of saying that the accounting system had become something of a shambles. In matters like this, you had to get it right and it was thought another year's profit would show a better graph.

It was at this crucial time that one of the most significant of all the names took over his role in the story of Stakis. With the finances in need of an overhaul, the man called in to sort them out was thirty-two-year-old Frank O'Callaghan, a working-class Glasgow lad with a burning ambition to succeed.

The eldest of six in the family of a steelworks foreman, O'Callaghan was born in a Dennistoun tenement before moving to the post-war housing scheme of Castlemilk. He took degrees in arts and accountancy and joined the small firm of Peacock and Henry before landing on the management consultancy side of McLintock, Moores and Murray. If he viewed this appointment as a springboard to finding a more challenging post within a company, he didn't have long to wait.

His first contact with Stakis was in that role of consultant, in anticipation of the Stock Market flotation, and it didn't take the boss long to decide that he wanted him on the staff. So Frank O'Callaghan took over as financial controller, embarking on a career which would run from 1972 till 1989, and making it clear from the start that he wanted to be a director within a year. He had no capital of his own but Reo Stakis lent him the money to buy shares.

O'Callaghan settled into the job, observing the ruling triumvirate of the time which consisted of Reo himself, John Loughray and a Cypriot called John Joakim, who worked mainly on the buying side and had become one of the family by marrying Xanthippi, sister of Harry Nicholas (owner of Renfrew's Glynhill Hotel) who was in turn married to Reo Stakis's sister Despina. The web of family connection was never-ending!

Regarding the financial confusion which had led to his appointment, O'Callaghan had the feeling that Reo Stakis was inclined to shoot the messenger and that there had been a reluctance to bring him the bad news when he should have been told it. Be that as it may, he was thoroughly enjoying his new job, acknowledging that Mr Stakis was very much the father figure and did not enter too closely into man-to-man relationships with his key executives.

To everyone in the company he remained "Mister Stakis" and O'Callaghan felt all others were minions. Despite the formalities, however, there were good open discussions between the boss and the two men who were now clearly his top lieutenants. In 1972 their respective ages were Reo, 59, John Loughray, 37, and Frank O'Callaghan, 32.

"Outwith the main organisation, the boss had his own property company of Ravenstone and I found he got on with his own job and trusted other people to get on with theirs," said O'Callaghan. "He would keep interference in business matters to a minimum and I cannot recall him ever saying 'No', at least not until much later, when he said it for the wrong reasons."

He was intrigued by the boss's methods: "He once bought a piece of land in Cornwall for £500,000 with the intention of building a hotel and leisure centre. I thought he should have waited until there was planning permission but his view was that he would then have had to pay a fortune for it. As it happened, he never did get permission but managed to sell it on nevertheless."

On another occasion, a lawyer who sought licences for the company in the Dumbarton area happened to mention an estate in County Kerry in the Irish Republic, for which a man in Dumbarton was bidding a fairly large sum. The Stakis ears were immediately pricked. Who in Dumbarton could afford that kind of money? Such an estate would surely become valuable if they discovered oil off the Irish coast? So he was interested and entered into a deal. The fact that it became a financial disaster at least left O'Callaghan comforted to know that the boss he was learning to revere was human enough to make mistakes.

As financial controller, he had the task of checking the boss's expenses, telling him what he could or could not put through. Stakis obeyed without a murmur. O'Callaghan also became aware of the total loyalty to his own community. They would all meet together at the Greek Orthodox Church on a Sunday, when families would naturally approach their leader about a job for one or other of their number.

Monday morning would be his time to inquire about a possible vacancy for one of his kinsfolk. He knew his people and trusted them implicitly which, in all truth, was more than his Scottish lieutenants could sometimes say. They had reservations about some of the Mediterranean imports who were foisted upon them.

22

SHARES IN DEMAND

That hiccup in bringing the company to the market a year earlier meant that they had rather missed the high shine of recent times. In 1972 they would have to take their chance in more uncertain conditions. A crisis in the docks and other industrial problems had hit the markets rather badly and there was a general feeling that the Stakis flotation could have been better timed.

One Glasgow stockbroker was giving the opinion that there would not be a tremendous demand from London, with plenty shares available for those who wanted them, even though the minimum purchase had been set at 500. That rather sour forecast could not have been further from the truth.

In fact, the offer was oversubscribed several times and had to be scaled down on the following basis: applications for 500 to 1200 shares received 250; applications up to 1500 received 300; up to 2500 received 500; up to 5000 received 1000; up to 500,000 received two per cent of the application and from 500,000 upwards, 15 per cent.

The name of Stakis was not widely familiar in England and the prospect of this Scottish-based company coming to the Stock Market had to be explained to many a Sassenach who could not imagine that it had grown out of a Highland clan.

Having held a Press conference in Glasgow, Reo Stakis went to show himself in London next day, presenting the flotation offer and, as ever, playing the effortless host of disarming ease and charm. He did, however, concede that he was not totally relaxed about accepting outsiders into his orbit.

"I won't say I have no regrets," he told journalists. "You always think you are losing part of your independence. But I am happy it will give the people who have helped to build up the group a chance to take part in its future."

The English getting to know about Reo Stakis for the first time were learning the intriguing story of his Cypriot background; of how he had arrived at Victoria Station, London, with that suitcase of lace and had since built up an empire which was reaching the Stock Exchange. It was the stuff of business romance.

He already employed 2500 people and knew a remarkable number of them by their first names. He confessed to only one luxury, his Rolls-Royce, which was used to convey him round eight or ten of his establishments on any one evening. He was talking with confidence about his empire, outlining the future with broad strokes on the map. "I believe in Scotland," he told the audience, confirming his loyalty to the adopted land. But now it was time to expand beyond its bounds.

The technicalities of the flotation were that Stakis was brought to the market via an offer of seven million ordinary 10-pence shares (out of a total 25 million) at a price of 36 pence. The family had retained a controlling interest of 60 per cent. The offer was made by Scottish Industrial Finance in association with brokers Rowe and Pitman and the Glasgow-based Speirs and Jeffrey. The profit record was substantial and solid, the pre-tax figure having climbed from under £14,000 ten years earlier to £570,000 for the year to October 1971.

The arrival of public status is remembered by Tony Lang as causing something of a culture shock in a company where the only people ever told about your profits were the bankers. From 1972 onwards things would be different.

But the company was doing well and the top team was in full flight. From the original twosome of Reo Stakis and John Loughray, always a close partnership, Donald Macdonald had worked his way up the ladder and the formidable Frank O'Callaghan was now on board. A management structure was being put in place, with the appointment of area managers, and the company was going to enormous lengths to improve the pension and employee-shareholding schemes.

Reo never forgot the part played in the flotation by people like George Reid, a director of the company and a partner in MacRoberts, the legal firm in Bath Street with whom he had maintained a close association. Another member of MacRoberts, Ludi Gardner, who was also Greek Consul in Glasgow, had been his personal lawyer, a role which would later be assumed by David MacRobert, the fifth generation of his family to serve the practice. Sadly, George Reid died in 1980—on his sixty-fifth birthday.

Life-long careers were being shaped for young men like Bill Mackay from Cardonald, who had served his apprenticeship in accountancy with William Duncan and Co, from where he became involved in the Stakis audit. He is unlikely to forget the experience. Indeed he still lives with the vivid memory of that day when the head of the audit team became overwhelmed by the task he was undertaking and literally took matters into his own hands. He walked off with the Stakis ledgers under his arm, crossed one of the bridges over the River Clyde—and dropped the lot into the water below!

It fell to young Mackay to hold the fort during the emergency and, if any good came out of the disaster, it was when Reo Stakis asked his friend Willie Duncan if Mackay would care to join the company. It was going to be less hazardous to put the audit on an in-house basis.

Bill Mackay would spend the next thirty-four years with the company, noting landmark occasions like gaining the franchise for the Kelvin Hall in Glasgow when it was the premier venue of its kind in Scotland. He recalled that the Scottish Motor Show, for example, brought the biggest rush of concentrated business ever known to a Stakis company. For ten solid days the volume of business absolutely astounded the catering staff, who had never had to work so hard in all their lives.

It was followed by the annual carnival, and memorable musical occasions such as the big-band visits of legends like James Last and his orchestra. The problem with the Kelvin Hall franchise was that business came in bursts and had none of the consistency which makes life easier.

If the boss was always to be known as "Mr Stakis, or later "Sir Reo," Bill remembered that the courtesy was returned. Until the latter stages of his career he would find himself invariably addressed as "Mr Mackay." Senior staff had the privilege of family weekends at places like Dunblane Hydro, where his children came to speak of "Uncle Reo."

"I had great respect for the man, even when I thought he was wrong," said Bill. "His fault, however understandable, was in treating the company as the family business long after it was not." Therein lay hint of a criticism which would surface at a later stage.

With the company now in the public domain, the outside world was taking notice and the financial analysts liked what they saw. The Stakis shares, having been offered at 36 pence with the flotation of June 1972, reached 44 pence but returned to the original price by January of the following year because of the Stock Market slump.

By then, however, they were announcing their first results since going public, with pre-tax profits of £656,000, which was higher than the forecast. With another year under the belt, the figures at

March 1974 showed that turnover had risen by £4 million to £13 million and profits were up to £841,000.

The influx of public money had brought an immediate mood of expansion, with a search for new hotel sites and the acquisition of more than seventy off-licence shops and forty betting shops. The off-licence business came directly from an approach by Bob Haddow, who was offering his chain while wishing to remain on the board.

That was no problem for Reo Stakis, who had a high regard for Mr Haddow, as well as for his son David, who ran the group and continued in that role with much success. In time, however, there was a good offer from Bass the brewers and the Haddow shops were sold on.

The company was now looking at a much broader canvas, contemplating ventures which would not have been possible under private ownership. Reo was even tempted to pursue an opportunity he had passed up in the early post-war years and break into shipping, in which others of his Greek nationality, most notably Aristotle Onassis, had become spectacularly successful.

He went as far as sending a friend to check out a ship at the Italian port of Brindisi. The venture was not followed through but it did remind him of that earlier opportunity to make a fortune. At the end of the Second World War, Reo Stakis had come to the aid of two Greek students who ran out of money while studying in Glasgow.

One of them, Andrew Spyrou, was staying as a guest in the Stakis home at the end of his course at the Royal College of Science and Technology, before it was Strathclyde University. One day he received a telegram from Aristotle Onassis, inviting him to join his business. Indeed, on his return to Greece, he became Onassis's right-hand man but did not lose contact with the family who helped him financially in Glasgow.

Onassis was already buying up the liberty ships which had been mass-produced by the Americans during the war and were now available for sale. It was into this potentially lucrative business that Spyrou was giving Reo Stakis an entrée. Those ships were on the market at £50,000 and in no time Onassis would be selling them for two or three million.

Andrew Spyrou, who married a Scots girl from Govan, was spending much of his time with Onassis in places like Monte Carlo, where he eventually made his home. Reo Stakis would look back and contemplate how big a shipping magnate he might have become.

He knew the offer was coming from a very honest young man— he was less impressed by the record of Onassis himself, strongly disapproving of the way he treated his famous lover, opera singer Maria Callas—and lived to regret not having taken up the golden chance. It may have been one of his biggest mistakes in business; then again, didn't he always believe in sticking to the things you know best?

He was never one to dwell too long on what might have been, however. His company was now in the public domain and there was one more key figure to enrol before the management structure was complete.

23

TRAGEDY OF ROYAL DARROCH

Stuart Jenkins was a King's Park boy, one of the four sons of an engineer at Weirs of Cathcart. Born in 1942, he was working as a young accountant in Glasgow when he was interviewed by Frank O'Callaghan for a job at Stakis, just at that critical point when they were preparing for the flotation.

The headquarters were still in the Chevalier building in Buchanan Street, though the plush restaurant was now closed. The casino upstairs had survived, not that Stuart knew anything about gambling. He simply got on with his job and by 1975 had been appointed chief accountant. His early observations were that Reo Stakis and John Loughray were very close but that Frank O'Callaghan was joining that top bracket, having brought some kind of order to what had amounted to financial chaos.

To him, Reo Stakis remained "the Boss" long after he had left his employment, such was his regard for a man who was fiercely loyal to those around him and who had a knack of persuading people to his own point of view. By 1976, however, Stuart Jenkins had decided this was not the job for him and left for pastures new. A year later he had a phone call from the Boss, who said he wanted him to come back and run the casinos. Jenkins, now beginning to feel himself more of a businessman than an accountant, was certainly tempted by the offer. So he accepted, while making it plain he didn't know the first thing about casinos. The Boss was confident he would get to grips with it.

So he entered upon a routine of life which started at nine in the evening and ran through till four o'clock next morning. It was a side of Stakis which was run mainly by people of Greek origin and somehow stood apart from the rest of the organisation.

With the approach of a new act, the Gaming Board had refused them a certificate because parts of the business were not being run strictly within the law. Five casino managers were suspended for giving credit, which they were not allowed to do. Jenkins was put in to sort out the situation and to expand it and, though he was entering unknown territory, his reward would be a place on the board when he achieved the aim.

He increased the number of casinos from nine to nineteen, moved the Chevalier from Buchanan Street to Hope Street and went to visit all 120 casinos in Britain to see which ones they should buy. Of that British total, nearly forty were in London and others were spread around places like Southampton and Bournemouth.

He attained that place on the board and was now becoming one of the top executive team which ran the company. This was a cash business and Reo Stakis knew only that it was a money-spinner. Jenkins' talents would be tested when the company had served its time in the provinces, with its middle-of-the-road gambling, and was ready to reach for higher spheres.

The significance of such a move could be gauged from the fact that, whereas the average spending of a gambler on a visit to a provincial casino was £50, the middle range of London casinos could count on £250 per head. This was what spurred Mr Stakis to arrange that meeting with the Waldock family at their Imperial Hotel in Russell Square, London. The Waldocks were substantial people who needed reassurance as to who they were dealing with. But the Stakis charm worked as ever and the family agreed to lease the premises which became the Regency.

If Stuart Jenkins had a criticism of the Boss it was that he didn't always give credit to an employee when it was due. He himself had gone to court to secure that London casino licence and thought it would not have been too much for the Boss to say "Well done!" Instead, he indicated that he knew all along they would get the licence. Similarly, if someone left the company, he suddenly became the wonderful chap he hadn't been before. Jenkins felt it came from a fear that people might get too big for their boots.

The casinos were an area where he had more than his share of approaches from the Boss about employing people of Greek origin; but he was building a team with a good mixture of British and Greek and gaining the respect of the latter in the process.

Many of the Stakis casinos had not opened during the afternoon, though gambling was permitted from 2pm till 4am. Jenkins moved towards afternoon opening, starting with lunch at midday.

Meanwhile, company secretary Tony Lang was not only looking after pensions and insurance but becoming involved in the buying of hotels as well. They had their eye on the Victoria in Nottingham, for which the asking price was £800,000. Stakis offered £680,000 and stuck to that price. In the absence of a buyer, it was put up for public auction and Lang was there to do the bidding, which started at £450,000. As others began to fall out, he put in a final Stakis bid of £635,000—and got it. It had been an old railway hotel and is still in the Stakis stable today. The business of getting licences was fraught with difficulty but it was Tony Lang's job to seek them.

The company had also moved into financial services, including stockbroking, buying a private investment bank in the Isle of Man, which was named Manin International after an ancient name for the island. It sent representatives to Gulf countries like Kuwait, where expatriates had money they could not spend. Manin would invest it for the day when they would return to the United Kingdom.

But that financial sector came unstuck in the Stock Market crash of 1987, when the monthly losses were running to £300,000.

On the question of insurance, it became the practice of many large companies in the early 1980s to take the responsibility in-house. Having totalled their premiums and made a few calculations, they discovered it would be cheaper to act as their own insurers. Stakis decided to follow this route, accepted a reasonable level of risk themselves and re-insured the rest to spread the load, all arranged by their own companies based in Bermuda and Guernsey.

They had had their share of misfortunes in the past, not least the disastrous fire which necessitated a major reconstruction of the Glasgow Grosvenor, but none of that prepared them for the calamity which broke on an October morning of 1983.

Reo Stakis was travelling in his car when he heard it on the radio. A massive explosion had ripped through his Royal Darroch Hotel on the outskirts of Aberdeen. Five people were dead and eighteen injured. He was driven straight to Aberdeen and couldn't believe the sight which met his eyes. "I never felt so unhappy in all my life," he said later.

Guests had been at breakfast in the ground-floor dining-room when a gas explosion blew out the front of the three-star hotel. Almost the whole of the ground floor collapsed twelve feet into the basement and the ensuing chaos was hard to comprehend. Flying debris crossed the car-park and reached the busy North Deeside Road, forty yards away, striking vehicles in the morning traffic.

Forty-one of the 67 bedrooms had been occupied the previous night and surviving residents joined 200 firemen, police, ambulance and medical staff as flames spread from one end of the building to the other. In the scene of utter devastation, it seemed quite miraculous that anyone at all had survived. Some guests were trapped in the debris, while others were able to scramble to safety from upper floors.

Among those who survived was Miss Linda Young, a public relations officer with Stakis, who was having breakfast with area manager John McFall when the blast went off. She explained: "John was sitting opposite me when he was blown twenty feet through the window into the hotel car-park. Incredibly, he was only slightly hurt and came back into the rubble to help me out."

When John Loughray phoned to say "The Royal Darroch has blown up!" Tony Lang had visions of some terrorist activity. But nothing so sinister, even if the tragedy was no less. The Gas Board was found responsible for the disaster.

In the mixture of guests and staff, the victims included 18-year-old Hazel Stirling, whose parents owned the Eagleton Hotel in Bridge of Allan. Others who died were hotel porter Stuart Walker, 44, of Craigielea Avenue, Aberdeen; Alister McKenna, 24, of Langlands Terrace, Bellsmyre, Dumbarton; Ian Gow, 49, of Dawson Avenue, Livingston, West Lothian; and Duncan Youngson, 40, from Hamilton. Mr Walker's wife Sylvia was among the badly injured, the couple having been the longest-serving members of the staff.

The Royal Darroch had been built by the well-known Aberdeen developer, Peter Cameron, who had to fight the stiff opposition of local people when he planned the hotel. Eventually he secured a licence and sold his Deeside hostelry to Stakis.

In the light of what happened, Reo had no stomach for rebuilding, believing that a tragedy of that kind would always have its associations. At a later stage, the site was used for the building of one of the company's Ashbourne Homes.

24

STAKIS SPICE?

The Stakis daughters had meanwhile grown into a glamorous quartet, with a talent as singers and musicians which bordered on professional standard. While Stassia was heading for a career as an actress, Rena, Ridi and Niki were playing guitar and keyboard and singing their way round festive occasions at home or during holidays in Greece.

They were covering the songs of Joan Baez, Bob Dylan and the Everly Brothers and were especially remembered for "The White Rose of Athens," the song which was a worldwide hit for their sister-Grecian, Nana Mouskouri. The girls were well aware of their father's deep pride in his daughters and didn't mind that they had become family ornaments worthy of display.

Reo might well have been tempted to sign up a cabaret act from within his own family and the prospect of a Stakis Spice was a thought to cause amusement in later years. With some professional guidance, it might not have been so much a flight of fancy.

Meanwhile, his glamorous girls were pursuing their various educational routes but with all the romantic instincts you would expect of young women. As the eldest of the four, Rena was privately petrified that the Greek tradition of arranged marriages might still survive to haunt her in the 1960s.

Such background thoughts affected her relationship with boys.

Adopting a modern view about the equality of the sexes—a view not shared in the Greek tradition—she had a horror of being landed with some older, more authoritative figure of a man.

"The taboos were scary," she said. "But if I was to marry, I was determined it would be for love and nothing else. I was a romantic. Because he had to struggle so hard to reach the top himself, my Dad wanted to see us married to people who had already reached their peak."

So Rena had read her father's mind and was well aware that he was trying to arrange her marriage. Again, the tradition was to remain within your own race so the sons of well-to-do friends would arrive from London or Athens or Cyprus for the obvious purpose of looking over the Stakis girls. What they saw was unlikely to turn them away since devastating looks were certainly a prime characteristic of the children produced by Reo and Annitsa Stakis.

People in high places, right up to the Archbishop in London, were discreetly enlisted to seek out suitable contenders. So the visiting prospectors were invariably the sons of good families, bred from gentlemen to become gentlemen themselves, though mostly ten years older or more. But the Stakis girls were not for choosing in the old-fashioned way and they politely but firmly resisted all romantic overtures.

Whatever may have been good for his own day, their father had the grace to accept that the times were quite clearly a-changing. His daughters would make their own choices, albeit aware in the privacy of their hearts that arranged marriage, according to the evidence of statistics, was every bit as likely to succeed as the union of free choice!

It was the principle that mattered, however, and that would at least grant them the freedom to make their own mistakes. In reality, of the five children who married, Rena, Ridi and Andros went through divorce, younger son Evros was separated and only

Niki escaped the pitfalls. The actress Stassia commuted in her film, theatrical and painting career between London and Los Angeles and stayed free of the bonds.

The girls were to discover that those long-standing traditions of the Greek nation were clasped far more closely to the bosom of exiles who had gone to Britain or the United States than to those who had stayed at home. It came as a surprise to find that in the homeland of Greek society they were keeping fairly much in line with the ways of the western world, for better or for worse.

After Laurel Bank School in Glasgow (now known as Laurel Park), Rena had been sent to the Swiss finishing school of Mont-Oliver in Lausanne, recommended by a friend of her father, through the Archbishop of the Greek Orthodox Church in London. In the year she left school, she had been more interested in the new BA degree in business administration but Switzerland was her destination and it was not an experience which brought her much joy.

The pupils were there mainly to learn French and the ones who were contented with their lot were those who could go home at weekends. There were no boys on the horizon and once again Rena felt repressed. From the age of seventeen she spent two years at the finishing school, gained her qualification for the ancient University of Nancy and went on to study languages at the Goethe Institute in Wiesbaden.

It was during this spell in Germany that she met Craig Anderson from Staten Island, who was serving with the United States Air Force in Wiesbaden. Rena had always missed the company of people of her own age, finding it difficult, because of the Greek tradition, to invite young people to her home in Glasgow.

Now she was keeping the company of the young American, having met him just three weeks before she was due to join the family for a holiday in Cyprus. Even in the short acquaintance, there was no doubt that the romantic Rena, by now aged twenty-two, had fallen in love with Craig Anderson. But passion would have to be suspended while she joined her parents in Famagusta, a city which was still open to Greeks in 1969, before the Turkish invasion of five years later.

What Rena did not bargain for, however, was the unexpected arrival of the young man from Staten Island. Following the love-trail to the Mediterranean, he made a beeline for Rena's father and ceremoniously asked for his daughter's hand in marriage! If Rena herself was stunned into silence, her father came much closer to apoplexy.

Reo and Annitsa had prided themselves in the strict morality of their daughters. They were expected to remain virgins. After all, their own mother had spent those wartime years in Cyprus, faithfully awaiting the moment when her Prince Charming would return from Britain to claim her hand. Her own father had seen to it that she remained out of reach to other men, so there would be no hint of gossip. Reo would be here once the war was over.

Times may have been a-changing but Rena knew that old habits die hard. She still shuddered at the memory of an incident at Dunblane, where the family had a holiday home in the grounds of the Hydro. At sixteen she had met a local boy and went walking and talking about the Beatles. It was all so innocent but someone had seen them and reported to her father.

He bided his time then called her in one morning, locked the door and grilled her about the association. What had been going on? It was the protectiveness of the caring father no doubt, based on assumptions about the Swinging Sixties which were often exaggerated far beyond reality.

From the innocence of Dunblane, Reo Stakis now had something far more serious on his hands. An American airman pursuing his daughter from Germany to Cyprus in the name of matrimony? Famagusta was full of United Nations soldiers but Rena was not giving herself a chance to meet anyone else, including the vast array of fine young Greeks who were of her own ethnic background.

Mr Stakis gave his advice, on the lines of that old saying about keeping apart for a year to see how it affects the relationship.

In the event, Rena left Wiesbaden and returned to Scotland, taking a job in her father's casino-restaurant at the Chevalier and giving herself at least some time to think things over. Now there was the temptation of forbidden fruit and when Craig Anderson turned up in Scotland, it was time to talk about marriage once more.

The wedding was planned for Dunblane Cathedral and a splendid affair it was. Craig's family came over en masse for the big day, including his mother, Marion Anderson, well-known in the Republican Party as a leading figure in the election of President Richard Nixon.

Reo Stakis had admitted defeat in guiding his first-born child to what would have seemed a suitable marriage; but he did so with good face and was now preparing to lead her down the aisle of Dunblane's magnificent cathedral. It was perhaps with no more than an impish sense of humour that he remarked to Rena on her wedding day that, if by chance she was not absolutely sure, there was still time to change her mind—and they could just have a party instead!

The Stakis intuition may well have been at work, however. For Rena was later to confess her true feelings on that wedding day. No sooner had she glided down the aisle on her father's arm, and seen the ring being placed on her finger, than she was struck by the awful truth that she had just made the biggest mistake of her life. Back at the Hydro, she rushed to her room to confront herself at the mirror with the ultimate dilemma of a young woman on her wedding day.

For the moment at least there was nothing for it but to continue with the charade. Married life would begin with her husband's parents in Staten Island, one of the boroughs of New York City, and while Craig went to college, Rena busied herself with an active life, taking a variety of jobs but also furthering her musical interest at New York University, with a long-held dream of writing music for the cinema.

There was much to engage her attention, not least in performing as a singer in a restaurant—and in landing the lead part in a New York production of Sandy Wilson's popular musical *The Boy Friend*.

On the Manhattan social scene there were fashionable balls to attend, much to do with raising funds for President Nixon and the Republican cause, all of which added up to a welcome diversion, while masking the fact that her marriage to Craig Anderson was collapsing. The doubts and fears of Dunblane had now properly firmed into reality.

So after four years in the United States she cut her ties, sacrificed the promise of a musical career and came home to Scotland. At least there were no children of the marriage, making it easier to break the bonds.

It was time to lick her wounds and where better to do so than in sunny Greece. Rena loved the sun, having always been conscious of the bleak Scottish weather and particularly the Glasgow smog. What is more, she was going to offer some support to sister Ridi, who was having her own marital problems.

Casting around that warm and pleasant land of her own people, Rena came to the conclusion that this was where she would like to spend her life. The fates may have been at work once more. Through friends of her brother-in-law, she met and fell in love with Efstathis Capoyanopoulos, a civil engineer—his name means "constant"—and despite the taboos about divorce in Greece, decided she was ready to settle down for a new start.

Family was important to Rena and so it was that she married Efstathis in 1977 and produced two sons, Andreas in 1978 and Reo two years later. From their home base in Athens, her husband established his own civil engineering business—and Rena found some kind of settled life at the age of thirty.

Ridi had married Vassilis Christopoulos, a handsome 22-year-old student from Athens, who was studying naval architecture at Glasgow University. They met when she was helping to organise classes in Greek studies and were married by His Eminence, Archbishop Athenagoras, at the cathedral in Glasgow, followed by a stylish reception for 400 at the Normandy Hotel.

At least Vassilis was of the same race, not that it made much difference to the success of the marriage—they were divorced some years later. Having changed her name to Christie after the divorce, Ridi returned to Scotland with her three children, earnestly needing something to occupy her time. Her father made a place for her in the Ravenstone property company which he ran outwith the main Stakis organisation, with offices first in Woodside Terrace and then at 144 West George Street. Ravenstone had very nearly gone to the market in the late 1970s, a move which was expected to bring in £37 million.

Building work was initiated all over Scotland and Ridi became a shareholder, along with her father, throwing herself into the task with enthusiasm and no doubt hoping to show an inherited acumen for business. In all truth, that was not exactly how it worked out. She had taken up an idea for building houses in Spain and that project went ahead at full steam, accumulating huge bills on travel alone.

Ridi herself was receiving a generous salary and expenses allowances but there was one snag: the Spanish houses were not selling. She remained the driving force behind Ravenstone, which was now launching into the bowling-alley business. But that proved to be the last straw.

Though Reo had dealt mainly with the Royal Bank of Scotland, lending for the Ravenstone schemes had come from two others, the Clydesdale and the Bank of Scotland, both of which were more than keen to have a contact with Stakis. Reo had given guarantees for indebtedness but matters reached a stage where those two banks took over the assets of the company and disposed of them. The Clydesdale and Bank of Scotland had in fact been extremely fair to Ravenstone. They could have been much tougher.

Despite the failure of selling houses in Spain, the family nevertheless became very fond of the country and to this day own a cluster of holiday homes near Marbella, at which as many of them as possible try to coincide for a summer break.

After the demise of Ravenstone, Ridi returned to Greece, where she launched herself into another business, dealing with imports from India. Her three children, daughters Rea and Anita and son George, went to Glenalmond School in Perthshire before going on to university.

Unlike Rena, Niki bypassed finishing school and remained in Glasgow, where she took a BA degree in economics and marketing at Strathclyde University, before her postgraduate years at London University, where she studied business and the teaching of English as a foreign language.

From the very beginning, therefore, it was clear she had inherited a taste for business and had a spell with her father as well as running a company outwith Stakis. She had a restaurant in Edinburgh and two in Glasgow and in partnership with brother Evros owned Benson's cocktail bar in the city centre. She had aspirations towards a proper foothold in the Stakis empire but there were those within the company who perceived a conflict of interests and pressed for her resignation. She disagreed completely but finally had to sever her connection.

For all the links with Cyprus, it is surprising to find it wasn't the regular habit of the Stakis family to go there on holiday. Niki had been to the land of her parents when she was very young and remembers only one other visit before she had a chance to know the island properly. By then she was twenty-five.

After university, she had gone to Greece in 1975, like Rena, to help sister Ridi through her divorce. She took a teaching post while there and was suddenly filled with an urge to see the land of her roots. So she crossed to Cyprus from mainland Greece on what was intended to be a two-day visit. There she was, playing the part of the typical tourist, taking photographs, when a group of local young people passed by, including one jaunty character who seemed to have a way with the girls.

Somewhat cheekily, he tried to have himself included in one of her snapshots, an intrusion she resisted before finally yielding to his charm and letting him into the frame. What she did not realise was that she was admitting him to the rest of her life. That two-day visit ended up as six weeks, during which the charming Evros Stylianides not only showed her around all the places she had heard about from her parents but had fallen in love with the dark-haired beauty who may have come from Scotland but shared his Cypriot heritage.

Niki's innocent stay at the Amathus Beach Hotel in Limassol had become a fateful adventure. Evros turned out to be in the business of wine and spirit manufacturing but at that moment was caught up in the uncertainty of his country, following the Turkish invasion when Greeks were driven out of Famagusta and President Makarios had been temporarily removed from office.

In the restoration of order, hordes of young Greek Cypriots were gathering in Limassol and the Amathus Beach became a focal point of their socialising. So Niki was back in the homeland of her parents at a highly poignant time, more and more aware of her roots and concluding that there was a good feeling in the air. She was trying to absorb the best from the cultures of both Scotland and Cyprus.

Meanwhile, back home there had always been the mixed blessing of having a wealthy father. Even at university, she was never allowed to forget who he was. Reo Stakis? You don't have to be here. You won't have to work! Reo and Annitsa were trying to give the kind of balanced upbringing that would enable them to cope with such pettiness.

All the time, Niki loved to hear about business from her father, by whom she was much influenced. If they were out on a Sunday run, when he would be casting an eye over properties, she was always interested in what he was doing, what he was saying.

Her mother was always the perfectionist, wanting everything to be right, to be clean. The house had to be in perfect order but she had no help in those early days and, with six children around her feet, it was a lot to expect.

Having now met her fate, Niki was married in 1981 and thought she would persuade her husband to live in Scotland. But Evros (same name as her young brother) was very much his own man and made it plain they would be living in Cyprus. Despite the ethnic links with the island, Niki had certain reservations about settling there. There was, she felt, a slight narrowness of outlook.

Evros, however, was not of that mentality, being notably free in his thinking and never putting any obstacles in the way of Niki being off home to see her parents. She settled into domestic life on the sunshine island, with her home in Limassol and a family of one boy and two girls to follow: Paris, Anita and Leana.

She found Cyprus an ideal environment for bringing up children, with a healthy, outdoor life, free spirited and without violence. She maintained a routine of visiting her parents two or three times a year and regretted only that she had not been able to follow a career of her own—and to keep a hand in the business, which is what she intended if she had still been living in Scotland.

If the Stakis girls had more than their fair share of film-star looks, the one who made a serious attempt at that career was Stassia. From early days she harboured dreams of being a dancer, a notion not discouraged by the fact that the family would go to the Waterloo Restaurant after church on Sunday and catch sight of the Tiller Girls, in Glasgow to appear at the Alhambra.

A first hint of what Stassia might do was gathered one day by Peter Balfour of Scottish and Newcastle, when he ran into Reo Stakis and commented on an uncharacteristically glum expression.

"I have a daughter who is going to bring disgrace on the family," he said. "She wants to be an actress."

"Well you can't really stop her," said Balfour, suggesting that he should instead try to encourage her into the Royal Scottish Academy of Music and Drama. Some time later, he met Reo again and the subject of Stassia cropped up. But still he looked glum.

"She got into the Academy," he said. "And she has won the gold medal."

Peter Balfour gathered that that brought an even bigger disgrace on the family! Stassia had indeed won the James Bridie gold medal and went on to a stage career in Scotland, London and Los Angeles, flirting on the fringes of films like the 1979 *Escape to Athena*, which had a Greek background and starred Roger Moore, David Niven, Elliott Gould, Telly Savalas and Claudia Cardinale.

Sometimes her cameo roles would survive the cutting-room, sometimes not. But she continued to carve an interesting life between London, New York and the Hollywood scene, making acquaintances such as Richard Gere and veering towards other outlets for her artistic urge, like screen-writing and painting. Through it all, she never lost her contact with ballet and still works out regularly.

On the business front, Stassia was regarded by some as having a limited awareness. There were occasions when she didn't even open letters which needed attention—and she would occasionally seek investment details which the advisers felt were unnecessary. Her father would always tell people to stick to the things they knew best and, in Stassia's case, that would have been acting, writing and painting.

Yet he was the first to acknowledge that his actress daughter did have a certain talent for the property market. She had bought and sold houses with good locations in London, New York and Los Angeles, sometimes renovating and renting them at the top end of the market and claiming that she had never made a loss. For those in any doubt about her acumen, the lady herself would retort quite sharply: "I have retained my wealth."

25

EXPENSIVE LESSON FOR EVROS

Evros Stakis, youngest of the family, went to Cambridge Technical College after school but did not follow it up with university. Instead he returned to Scotland, joined his father's company for some work experience and enjoyed the personnel department but not much else. The whole corporate idea was too regimented for Evros, who was a bit of a free spirit, maybe even a loose cannon. The very idea of wearing a suit went against the grain and even approaching forty he was claiming he hadn't worn a tie for years.

His boredom reached the point of rebellion after John Loughray decided the boss's son needed some discipline and sent him to work at the Royal Darroch Hotel in Aberdeen. Asked to count the crockery, Evros plugged in his personal stereo and instead of counting plates, cups and saucers he began to smash them. So that was the end of that, supporting an earlier reputation for being a young man of action, even at school, where he would counteract the bullies by organising a gang to sort them out.

He had not had his troubles to seek at Glasgow Academy, where he reckoned he was victimised by teachers as well as boys. Alleging that he was beaten up by one particular teacher, he gives a graphic description of how he was dragged by the hair into another room and had his head bashed against a blackboard, emerging in a state of total shock. All round, he felt, there was a jealousy of his father's success, which might have been real. On the other hand, Evros might have been oversensitive to the racial difference.

He had good friends in Pollokshields where he lived, boys like Ronnie Somerville, a surgeon's son, Dougie Walker, Dougie Anderson and John Sinclair. But from his earliest days he knew there was a difference; he was not just part of another Glasgow family.

"Mum was brilliant and made sure we were well groomed and that we respected people," said Evros. "I was able to communicate with Mum but not so much with Dad. I'm still closer to her. It is only in more recent times that I have been able to open up with Dad and tell him things."

After that Royal Darroch episode of smashing crockery, Evros headed for the American University of Athens and came away with a degree in history, having written a thesis on the subject of Northern Ireland and Cyprus, two islands which didn't have their troubles to seek. After university, Evros was fired with the idea of setting up a gallery for the new wave of Russian art, having been inspired by the work of George Costaki. That came to nothing, however, and he turned instead to music.

From his teenage years in the mid-1970s, friends remembered that Evros could talk of little else but the pop group Queen, led by Freddie Mercury. If his thoughts were turning to a career in the music business, however, the main inspiration of his life was now David Bowie, the rock singer from Brixton who diverted from an early intention to being a Buddhist monk towards a music career in which he became the high priest of weird and outrageous performance.

Evros played the saxophone but not with any thought of being a top performer himself. Instead, following the family bent for organisation, he wanted to produce and stage the musical events, to make things happen. His actress sister Stassia had been the girlfriend of Frank Musker, a talented songwriter who had worked with Bette Midler and Air Supply and wrote for Scotland's Sheena Easton.

Musker was looking for an investor with whom he could set up a music publishing company and Evros Stakis appeared on his horizon, ready-made, furnished with his share of the family fortune to use as he decreed. In retrospect, he believed it was a big mistake to let loose a young man with all that money and no experience of how to handle it.

That opportunity to handle it arose through trusts set up by Reo's lawyer, Hugh McCalman, by which the youngsters received significant blocks of shares in the company, amounting to a large part of their inheritance in advance.

So Evros became involved with Frank Musker in a company they called FM Songs, set up in 1984. They had such clients as John Denver, Memphis and Bucks Fizz, which meant he was dividing his time between London and Los Angeles, not unlike Stassia. On the American side he stayed at the beach end of LA, on Santa Monica's Ocean Boulevard, and found that his naturally charming and gregarious manner soon brought him a circle of friends on the fringe of the Hollywood scene.

Madonna used to drop round to his house at a time when clever promotional work had thrust her into that slot of role-model for the young. Evros was a guest at her wedding to Sean Penn and was soon known to most people, from film producer Oliver Stone to actress Jodi Foster and superstar pop singer Prince, then attracting much controversy for his tendency to mix religious and sexual themes in his music.

To Evros it was the excitement of gaining an entrée to a glamorous world of film and music, where his disarming good looks which had brought him such success with the girls in Glasgow would stand him in good stead amidst the froth and flotsam of Tinseltown.

But the partnership with Frank Musker was not working out. While Evros acknowledged the man's talents, he did not like what he was doing with the company. As the one who provided the money, he put it bluntly: "I got rid of him! We were spending a lot but I didn't think he was doing things the right way. What was 'hip' was coming from me."

Evros remained in music publishing, teaming up with Trevor Lawrence, who was producing acts like the Pointer Sisters. In 1992 Evros's company published Jimmy Nail's No 1 single "Ain't No Doubt," which was nominated for the Ivor Novello Award. He also provided solo artistes for the *Riverdance* success as well as for the film *Rob Roy*.

But despite touching base with success, the final outcome of his involvement in the musical world was quite disastrous. In short, he lost a fortune, which ran into several millions. He shrugs in acknowledgement of the disaster and puts it down to the fact that he let other people's creativity take over and didn't believe sufficiently in himself. For Evros it was a case of what might have been. If only they had signed the Pet Shop Boys when they had the chance to do so, they would have made the millions instead of losing them.

In 1996, having leaned more and more towards the cinema, he set up Stirling Films UK Ltd, taking the name from that historic town near his parents' home, which gained worldwide attention from the Mel Gibson film *Braveheart*. With screen-writer and producer Jack Cameron Bond, he began to develop feature films and documentaries as well as television dramas. They were low-budget productions in wider cinematic terms but still required funding to the extent of three or four million.

Nowadays Evros bases himself in London, with a home in Kensington and a suite of offices covering five floors in Museum Street, at the other end of Oxford Street. There is a basic staff of thirteen which can rise to eighty or ninety when they move into production. Despite his massive losses, the Stakis family have backed him in his latest venture. He finds that the Stakis name still opens doors.

A chastened Evros accepts his own share of responsibility for what happened in his earlier days but, for all his deep affection for his father, he still maintains it was a mistake to put so much money into young hands.

"I am not a playboy," he assures you. "I work hard and I don't mess around. But it was wrong to put that burden on young people who were not trained to handle it. I wouldn't do that with my own children."

On the other hand, his father had anticipated that any son of his would surely be blessed with fundamental shrewdness. His criticism of Evros, in retrospect, was that he didn't have the ability to judge the people with whom he was involved.

Evros married a top model, Debbie Mudd, daughter of pop-star Fred Mudd and Leila Williams, a former Miss United Kingdom and one-time presenter of *Blue Peter* on television. Evros's marriage came unstuck but even in separation they remained good friends and Evros secured a singing contract for his estranged wife.

He claims that he set out to make a success of his business, not with a drive to prove anything to his father but simply to prove himself to himself: "I now have the confidence I didn't have before. All I need is a bit of luck."

Then he revealed a secret ambition, somewhat in contradiction of those earlier days when he didn't feel he had any part to play in the empire his father had created so successfully:

"When I am older, I would like to participate in the Stakis organisation, to play my part in keeping the family name to the fore. Rupert Murdoch has shown how it can be done, to bring in your family in a way that they can gradually take over the running of the empire."

For Evros, in the light of events which led to the 1999 take-over, it proved no more than a pipe-dream. Once again, it was a case of what-might-have-been. He says: "If Dad had brought my brother Andros and me in together I think the formula would have worked. Everyone seems to fear nepotism but there is nothing wrong with bringing in your own family. You surely know their character.

"Andros has a habit of shouting and screaming at people. Well, he could have screamed at me instead. I would have been the buffer because my temperament is different. I never lose my temper and I am more diplomatic than Andros. It would have been good for him to have had me there. He has a very good business mind but I get along much better with people."

It was Andros alone, however, who was to be groomed in time for the responsibility of fulfilling his father's ambition. Reo Stakis had no greater wish than that his elder son would carry forward a proud name and that he would, one day, be installed at the head of the family empire.

26

ANDROS JOINS THE FIRM

The focus of the family's future in business would fall almost wholly upon Andros, elder of the two sons, fifth of the six children. From his early consciousness he was aware that his father was someone special—head of the Greek community in Scotland, friendly with archbishops, important in business. There was something intimidating in all this.

Mother's philosophy was that the image of the family was related to the tidiness of the house, so they were not supposed to run around and get dirty, but they did so just the same.

Despite his father's success in life, Andros noticed he had never lost the common touch. On their visit to a Cyprus village he was intrigued to watch as Reo stopped to speak to a poor old lady who was hanging out her washing. They talked like soul-mates, without a hint of any difference in status, and the two of them were completely at home with each other.

That ability to reach out to people was something Andros admired as a great strength in his father. Yet he was puzzled by the fact that he seemed unable to do the same thing with his own children. Perhaps it was easier to talk to strangers.

There was one area, however, in which Andros felt he bonded completely with his father and that was in shooting. "On those occasions everyone tends to treat you like an adult," he explained.

"But that was the only time Dad gave me responsibility as a young man. I used to shoot with him and his friends when I was at university and there I was, aged seventeen, with my long hair and expounding left-wing politics, holding a gun while denigrating his group of people for being right-wing capitalist fascists!

"I was sympathising with Third World countries being ripped off by multinational companies. At Edinburgh University I had left-wing teachers so you can understand why Dad and I didn't have a good dialogue at that time."

Andros felt he had to prove himself at university, otherwise people would say he didn't have the ability. But his academic record was sound and he was tempted to further reinforce it by taking a doctorate.

Privately, he was concerned by the fact that his father had had a heart scare. If anything happened to him, who was going to deal with the family interests? His own life so far, he concluded, had been a race against time, like getting to university as quickly as possible. He had dreamed of going to Oxbridge, which he felt would have helped his confidence. He had thought of an officer's training course at Sandhurst but he had just turned seventeen. So he settled for a B.Comm. at Edinburgh University, still torn between the academic world and learning about the business.

After Edinburgh, he joined Stakis for a year of work experience and was amused that people were spending so much time trying to decide what title he should have.

"I was a sensitive kid but I knew that, intellectually, I was as capable as any of them," he recalled. "They were trying to put me in a bracket so they would know which car to give me and what miserable salary to offer. Frankly, I didn't give a damn.

"The only part of the company I enjoyed was the casino division, where there was a good atmosphere and they treated me nicely. But I sensed from day one that I was not welcome at Stakis. John Loughray was my father's right-hand man but even he seemed to regard me as a potential threat. What I do remember about John, however, is that he was a brilliant card player, a man who could work things through very patiently. Dad had his corps of people around him and worked a great deal through John."

That spell in the company was just an interlude for Andros, who thought the best training he could receive would be at America's top school. So off he went to Cornell University, which lies in a beautiful setting near Rochester in upstate New York. It is regarded as the Eton of the hotel business, the place to which everyone in the industry aspires, and that was where Andros did his Masters in hotel administration, a kind of MBA with specialisation.

There he was exposed to the technology of the future at a time when we were lagging behind in this country. He now knew for sure that it was the Americans who had revolutionised the industry, bringing it into the modern era with their Hiltons, Sheratons, Marriotts, Four Seasons and Hyatts, often with their atrium designs.

From Cornell he stayed on in North America and joined Hilton, enrolled in the general management training programme in Montreal by Charlie Bell, the president, who was known to both his father and John Loughray. At Cornell they had also been trained in hotel architecture and Andros later went on to gain practical experience with Burman Bouchard, a well-known firm of architects, still based in Montreal.

Cornell had been a real eye-opener, using the apparently ruthless method of breaking you down, as if you were a nobody, before building you up in their own image. You learned discipline and finally you emerged with a confidence which Andros had never known before.

With a feeling of inner strength, he came back to Scotland in 1980, at the age of twenty-four, ready and eager to join the Stakis organisation. Once again there was some scurrying to find a suitable slot for the boss's son, while he himself was trying to decide what he would prefer.

"I didn't want to work in the hotel division because I didn't like the style of the man in charge, Donald Macdonald. It smacked too much of autocratic management. So I devoted myself to the property side, basically taking over those Stakis properties which were not being used or developed and grouping them together in an attempt to maximise their profit."

If the story of Stakis was to become one of bitter personal feuds by the end of the 1980s, the first seeds of conflict were sown at the start of that decade with the arrival of Andros as a full-time executive.

"The hostility I faced from everyone was nothing short of hell," is how he remembered it at a distance of nearly twenty years. "I used to go to work crying. Yes, I would actually be in tears when I was leaving for the office. I felt my father was not listening and he didn't see what was happening in little cliques behind his back. There was a power situation developing."

Was he not over-reacting in anticipation of some hostility to his privileged position?

"Of course I was the boss's son and they had no desire to listen to my new ideas. They were out to put me down. At every turn they found ways of discrediting me, attacking me from all sides. I respected Frank O'Callaghan as a corporate accountant and never pretended to be in his class in that respect. But I found him to be negative in other ways. In America, I had learned that the standard method of judging the performance and growth of a company was through earnings-per-share, whereas at Stakis it was profits-before-tax which was the main yardstick."

Therein lay a major difference between Frank O'Callaghan and Andros, who would subsequently point out that the former idea was now the accepted way of judging a company in the United Kingdom.

The dynamic young man, fresh from his academic background and American training, was bristling with ideas and making known opinions which were not likely to win friends. For example, he announced to a board meeting that he wouldn't be seen dead in a Stakis pub!

"We were designing them in the way they had been doing for years—the kind of places with orange bulbs everywhere," he said. "Coming back from America, I could see we were decades behind. So I went up to Glasgow School of Art and asked students to design the type of place I would like to see for a pub we had in Pollokshaws Road.

"We spent £80,000 on that concept and I was there on the opening night, hoping all would go well. Within a month that place was doing £16,000 a week turnover and was soon rocketing above that.

"That started the ball rolling for refurbishment, which didn't cost a lot. I said I wanted responsibility and John Loughray asked me to redesign the steakhouse at the Pond Hotel in the west end of Glasgow. Actually we didn't make so much money out of the steakhouses but they had enabled the company to become well-known, with the idea that we had changed the eating habits of Scotland. In fact, within the company there had been an ongoing debate as to whether they should be turned into pubs."

Given the project at the Pond, Andros had already studied in America a concept called Charthouse, which involved the effective use of glass. Around the same time, Glasgow had seen the opening of the building to house the Burrell Collection and, with these thoughts in mind, he set an architect to work. When he returned from a visit to America, however, he found that, on the site of what he was planning, they were putting in a swimming-pool!

"I got no warning; wasn't consulted," he said. "Dad tended to take the side of the managers so he and I did not always agree.

"But because we had the property interest in common, he would

160

take my side in these matters when the others were repudiating my ideas. They did that until I brought in David Aspin, who was so far ahead of them in that field that they left us to start the new division, Stakis Land and Estates."

David Aspin had been with Jones Lang Wootton, the chartered surveyors, but came directly from Guardian Royal Exchange, having been recommended to Andros. He was an Englishman of much charisma, strongly championed by the boss's son, who claimed that other executives were jealous of Aspin and that they were just amateurs by comparison.

Andros was certainly given to straight talking. He said his property division was creating £1 million of profit yet they hadn't given him a secretary. The only finance at his disposal, he said, had to come from money raised by selling property and exploiting sites.

He wanted to build hotels at a time they were too expensive to buy, saying the company had to look ahead. But he found himself in opposition to John Loughray and Donald Macdonald and accused them of preferring to buy "useless ones and doing them up."

Despite the growing difference between himself and his father's trusted lieutenants, Andros was on the main board of Stakis and speaking confidently to journalists in the mid-1980s. It was only a matter of time before they took off, he said, envisaging the company getting twenty-five times bigger and moving more and more into property development.

It was in keeping with the mood of the time, when inflation seemed set to continue unabated—and before the horrors of the Stock Market crash of 1987. Andros had been raised in an atmosphere of big business and as he was enthusing about the future, his father was joining in the interview to contemplate the succession and to say: "My main object is to see that the company grows; so the right man must come in.

"If Andros proves that he is that right man then I shall be happy to see him carry on. He has more than twenty-five years of a start on me but he is showing that he has the business instinct. He is ambitious and has imagination and flair. Being the son of a successful person is not easy but, at twenty-nine, the indications are that he is of the right calibre. I'm glad that he is respected by the board."

Whatever the evidence of that respect, it was not to survive for long. Andros had had his say. But there was another side to the story.

27

FRICTION AT THE TOP

Though the Stakis company had gone public in 1972 and the team of top management was securely established, it was not unnatural that the founder should harbour dreams of a continuing family connection.

So when Andros arrived on the scene in the early 1980s it seemed like the first step in what his father hoped would be a steady progression to the top, where he would one day succeed as chairman. Of course history would teach that successful fathers are seldom followed by successful sons, the very expectation in itself providing a hurdle to a successor who may or may not be cut out for the job.

The notion that "He's not the man his father was" has become a well-worn cliché, even when the young man has all the potential to succeed but has not yet had time to prove it. Like everyone else, Reo Stakis had observed the recent history of the House of Fraser, where the young Hugh Fraser had to fill his father's shoes when only twenty-eight, and was on a hiding to nothing in the footsteps of such a dynamic figure as the late Lord Fraser of Allander.

Young Hugh, as he inevitably became known, was not without his talents, hard-working, compassionate to the point of giving many a helping hand but forced into a top position in British business at an age when some of his father's rivals were simply waiting to crucify him.

He had not helped himself by falling victim to that gambling addiction, nor with some highly-publicised romances, one of which ended tragically. And when he did falter, it was much in the predictable manner. Nevertheless, his early death revealed a great public warmth and sympathy for an essentially decent if vulnerable human being.

Reo Stakis hoped he would have better luck with his own offspring and set out to give elder son Andros every opportunity to prove himself a worthy successor. He discussed with financial director Frank O'Callaghan how they could place the young man within the company.

In the purchasing of hotels and pubs, there was frequently a piece of land or property within the deal which did not fit in with requirements, leaving an assortment which could be sold or rented. There were even steakhouses, not doing so well, which could be leased out—and from all of this it was decided to form a property division, which was run initially by company secretary Tony Lang and had a rent-roll of £300,000 a year.

With the hotels and casinos showing little enthusiasm for engaging the boss's son, Tony Lang found himself faced with a decision that Andros Stakis would take charge of the property wing. He stepped aside to accommodate the young man but felt he had witnessed the first sign of the dynastic problem. This was where Andros would seek to develop his credibility in the business but Lang had his doubts; and he was not alone.

The four trusted lieutenants who surrounded Reo Stakis were putting Andros under close scrutiny, no doubt seeking to assess what threat he might pose to their respective positions. His elevation to the main board aroused apprehension in those top four, John Loughray, Donald Macdonald, Frank O'Callaghan and Stuart Jenkins.

Their feelings were summed up by Macdonald, who made the analogy of the executives being four experienced climbers who reach the top of the mountain and are joined by this chap who steps out of a helicopter and has no idea of what happened between the foot of the mountain and the top. "You couldn't discuss the terrain with him because he hadn't been there," is how he put it.

If Andros had not "been there," as far as experience was concerned, he defended himself by saying he had gone through the very best training imaginable so that he could make a positive contribution to the group.

Andros took over the property company and again faced the frowns of the executives who claimed he did not inspire confidence with his deals. He, in turn, accused those critics of jealousy and, even with the hindsight of years, would declare himself incredibly proud of those deals, whether it was the acquiring of the highly successful St Anne's Manor at Bracknell, buying out the freehold of the St Ermin's in London or selling the Pond Hotel in Glasgow.

Whoever was right, Andros was bristling with ideas, not least the one which said they should move into the private nursing-home business which was just beginning to develop. It seemed a sensible suggestion and the Ashbourne Homes have survived to prosper, though no longer under the Stakis umbrella.

They were run by an old school friend of Andros, Tom Hamilton, who led a management buy-out for £50 million. They were then floated on the Stock Market a year later at £85 million, with Hamilton making a million and remaining as chief executive when American interests took over and merged Ashbourne with a US group.

Problems arose when, in the need to finance these capital projects, the bigger banks refused to match the lower rates on offer from a string of smaller banks, which were anxious for a share of the Stakis action. However wisely, the company then accepted those lower rates.

The four lieutenants were becoming increasingly alarmed by events, feeling Andros was not cut out for the job. While conceding he was a personable young man, they became uncomfortable with a succession of minor matters. If a board meeting started at 9.30am, for example, it was not unusual for Andros to arrive half an hour late, not in any apologetic manner but full of bounce, with hair a-flying, in a way which drew disapproval from everyone, including his father.

There were certain codes by which executives conducted their activities but these did not seem to apply to Andros. Whereas the group managing director was allowed a Mercedes, the lesser mortal who was now running the property company for Andros, the charismatic David Aspin, was favoured with a Porsche and would fly off in Concorde for routine trips to America.

Rumblings of discontent were soon mounting among senior men who had grown to know Reo as a man of modest spending, never a skinflint but equally not one to favour ostentation. The memory of peasant days in Cyprus, when his father's debts were a source of worry, were far too vivid for him to lose the perspective of what a lifestyle should be.

So the doubts and suspicions and the conflicts began to mushroom, more or less in tandem with the mounting confidence of Andros, who became more expansive the longer he was in the job. The internal critics felt the group was supporting his various ventures in property and giving them the aura of good deals when they were not.

Andros was spending money as no-one else would have dared and there was a succession of managerial blow-ups. The ingredients of conflict were as obvious as they were traditional. The boss's son, with the brashness of youth, comes in through the door of privilege and raises resentment in older men who are there on merit.

Caught in the midst of the wrangling, Reo was naturally torn between love of his son and loyalty to the men who had helped to build the Stakis organisation to its position of pre-eminence. He dearly wanted to see Andros emerge as a proven successor and would encourage his moves in property. To the extent that he knew something of the bad blood now running between his son and the top men, he felt the latter were gunning for Andros and making life difficult for him.

Yet, curiously, his knowledge of the bitter infighting turned out to be limited. He later challenged Andros as to why he had not consulted him about his problems. Andros replied that he wanted to prove his independence and did not wish to be running to his father the moment a problem arose.

For all their devotion as a family—and there was a tendency not to see the faults in each other—there would be furious rows between Reo and Andros. When these erupted, the pair of them would switch into the Greek language in which Reo was naturally more fluent and in which they could both express themselves with more assurance. With the whole family completely fluent in the traditional tongue, it was Greek which had always taken precedence in the home.

As father and son proceeded to air their differences in a "foreign" language, however, other key men in the hierarchy came to resent this form of exclusion. They would also take to pondering the situation of Andros and find no sign of his parents in his demeanour—he could display an arrogance of which there was absolutely no trace in either Reo or Annitsa. They were both quiet, modest people, brought up in a peasant tradition which set the tone of their life-long behaviour.

Having raised their children respect their own traditions, there seemed only one possible explanation for the more volatile trait and that was that Andros had been exposed to the harsher attitudes of the western world through his Glasgow childhood.

Either that or he had not learned to control his emotions in the same way as his father; because, although Reo was known for his quiet demeanour, he held just as forceful opinions and burning passions as his more voluble son.

But something had gone seriously wrong at this point in 1985 and as Reo Stakis became more aware of it, he arranged an excursion to Cyprus in the hope of improving relations. The hotels boss, Donald Macdonald, and financial director Frank O'Callaghan would bring their wives, Christine and Elizabeth, and the party would be completed with Reo and Andros. From their base at the Amathus Beach Hotel in Limassol they were treated like royalty, joining the boss on his return to Kato-Drys, where they met some of his old school friends and the hospitality flowed freely.

Donald Macdonald observed the scene and was touchingly reminded of his own background and upbringing in the Western Isles of Scotland, where the return of a local hero would evoke a similarly quiet pride. It was all fruit and cake and no strong drink required to stimulate the warmth of natural conversation.

Macdonald noticed, however, that one person was mostly missing from these happy celebrations. Andros was off doing something else and, instead of cementing relations, this Mediterranean visit had rather the opposite effect. Much as it had been a wonderfully luxurious holiday, he felt it had been disastrous from the human friendship point of view.

He came home from that adventure with an uneasy feeling that the writing was on the wall. Within the company there were those who felt the only hope was that Andros would just decide to leave. With hindsight, Donald Macdonald said "The responsible thing for us would have been to dismiss him. But that would have meant a public fight with Reo and that would also have been disastrous. I think Andros's heart was certainly in the business but he didn't understand it. He didn't understand people and he had a knack of gathering the wrong ones around him."

Whatever the differences between Andros and his father, how-ever, Reo came strongly to his son's defence in matters like acquiring good sites and introducing successful concepts, such as the Country Court Hotels, which owed their existence entirely to the Andros philosophy. They added value to the company and the irony is that, otherwise, the Stakis organisation might not have attracted the interest of Ladbroke and its Hilton International group.

28

BOARDROOM COUP?

As well as the Andros factor, there were those who thought that his father had not been so sharply focused on the business since his heart scare a few years earlier. The facts were that Reo, who had always been a fit and healthy man—he was a keen tennis player among other things—was struck down by a heart attack in 1982 and did not want the world to know about it. There is a long-standing, if irrational, tradition among people of strong character to equate illness with weakness.

On top of that, the public had a habit of getting matters of health very quickly out of proportion so, all in all, the less they knew the better. In loyalty to his father, Andros was putting about the story that Reo was out of the country when in fact he was lying in the intensive care unit of Glasgow Southern General!

Even Annitsa recalls a night when she thought he was away on business; in fact her husband had taken unwell and, to save her alarm, had booked himself into hospital.

She was already accustomed to his habit of keeping business affairs out of the domestic conversation and close to his chest. She smiles wryly about travelling in the old tram-cars and overhearing Glasgow wifies saying "Oh it's that Stakis again." Something would have appeared in the newspapers, perhaps another restaurant planned, a hotel deal completed, but for Annitsa this would be the first she had heard of it!

She would question him at teatime, only to have the tram-car gossip confirmed as truth. Similarly, the children would come home from school with titbits about the family business, which was still news to them.

Now, however, there were rumblings about Reo's own future, of which even he had no knowledge. Matters came to a head on 26th March 1986 when the other directors met at the home of Frank O'Callaghan in Hamilton Avenue, Pollokshields, in what had all the elements of a boardroom coup. The participants were not only the key executives, including secretary Tony Lang, but two non-executive directors, the Glasgow insurance broker Sir Peter Hutchison, who had been around since 1979, and Mr Graham Lewis, former managing director of the hotels division at Grand Metropolitan.

In essence, the collective view was that Reo Stakis should stand down as chairman and that Andros should somehow be shackled. The business would then come under the control of John Loughray, who commanded widespread respect within the company but had never pushed his own case, not even in this crucial instance.

Indeed, there had been an occasion shortly before when Reo, with thoughts of the succession, seemed to be paving the way for Loughray to become chairman—on the understanding that he in turn would champion the cause of Andros succeeding him. A fiercely ambitious man would have jumped at the chance but Loughray felt unable to give any such guarantee.

At the end of that dramatic meeting the general understanding was that Sir Peter and Graham Lewis, as the outside figures, would meet the chairman face to face and deliver the board's request. Instead, they put it all down in a letter which was delivered through his door. It was the wrong way to do it.

Reo Stakis was deeply upset and now regarded Loughray and

O'Callaghan as traitors. He commented to Macdonald, a man he had always liked: "I was brought up in the country and know that, if you put a young cockerel into the farmyard beside the hens, the old cockerels will try to kill it." The inference was that Andros was the young cockerel.

With that meeting taking place in O'Callaghan's house, it was the financial director himself who became chief suspect. The others spring to his defence, however, and say the venue was chosen merely for convenience. Whether a personal visit from Hutchison and Lewis would have made any difference is a matter for speculation. Frank O'Callaghan found that Reo was not inclined to talk to any of them after that, but he suspected he had taken the matter to heart nevertheless.

There were now signs that his thoughts were turning towards the succession, perhaps securing a non-executive chairman who would keep the seat hot for Andros and guide him to the responsibility in the manner which Loughray could not guarantee.

The name which came to the fore was that of Professor Roland Smith, an English academic who had become a prominent figure on the wider business stage, with an assortment of responsibilities which included at that point the chairmanship of Manchester United.

With uncertainty still hovering over the house of Stakis, Donald Macdonald was due to go on holiday at the end of July 1986, flying off to Disney World in Florida with his wife and children. Returning to Manchester Airport on 23rd August, he was driving north when he stopped for petrol at Gretna and happened to buy a *Glasgow Herald*. His eye landed on a headline which struck him like a bolt from the blue. Roland Smith was the new chairman of the Stakis organisation.

The process had begun just two days after his departure when Reo called a board meeting with the proposition that he would stand aside in favour of Professor Smith. Whereas the board was in the habit of reaching decisions by consensus, this one had gone to the vote and the absence of Macdonald was crucial. Reo and Andros lined up with Graham Lewis and Sir Peter Hutchison to give them a single-vote majority over John Loughray, Frank O'Callaghan and Stuart Jenkins.

John Loughray, who would have been the popular choice, was then earning £90,000 a year on a full-time basis whereas the professor was being brought in for a two-day week at £100,000 a year, plus a Jaguar and driver.

Macdonald was upset that the meeting had been called in his absence but reckoned that Smith had been recruited to support Andros and prepare for the sacking of John Loughray. A week or so later, by coincidence, Loughray, Macdonald and Jenkins were all in London on business and took the opportunity to have a frank discussion on what they could do about Smith.

Macdonald told Loughray that if he was prepared to stand up against Reo over the appointment, he would put his own job on the line and back him, to the point of going public and declaring that the executive directors of Stakis didn't want Roland Smith as chairman. Jenkins said he was prepared to do the same.

By the end of that week, John Loughray had sought legal advice on what they could do to scupper the appointment. O'Callaghan and Lang were now putting together a plan of action in readiness for a board meeting due on Thursday, 18th September.

With his faith steeped in the Free Church of Scotland, as befitted a man from Harris, Donald Macdonald had every belief in miracles. He could have been excused for thinking the hand of God itself was intervening in the affairs of the Stakis organisation with the news which reached his ears. Whereas voting at the board meeting would present a precarious balance, he now learned that Sir Peter Hutchison would be safely absent. In fact he would be hopelessly out of contact in an emergency, deep in the heart of the Orient on the mission of gathering rhododendrons, on which he was a specialist.

29

THE VITAL VOTE

On the Sunday before the board meeting, Macdonald had a call from the boss, inviting him round to see him. Both men lived in Dunblane. He was on the point of taking his children to Sunday School and going on to church himself so he said he would pop round after lunch.

Macdonald thought the boss had discovered what was afoot but instead he was handed a letter thanking him for his services during Reo's chairmanship. Now, Reo said, it was time to install Roland Smith in the chair and to get rid of John Loughray.

Making clear his displeasure, Macdonald said the company's greatest strength would become its biggest weakness if Loughray went.

"What do you mean?" asked Reo.

Said Macdonald: "Look at that wall. If you take a lintel out of the door, one half of the wall will go with it. The fact that we have all been brought together by you and have grown up together means that the moment John Loughray goes, you cannot stop the structure from crumbling. It will shake the company to the core."

That vital board meeting took place four days later, when all hell broke loose. As anticipated in the absence of Sir Peter Hutchison, the balance of power now lay with the Big Four, who promptly carried through their plan to remove Professor Smith even before he had arrived. But they took it one stage further and told Reo Stakis that they wanted him to resign as chairman.

He could not believe what he was hearing. But his ears did not deceive him and the management group was ready to put it to the vote. In the circumstances, Reo had no option but to stand down, whatever else might happen when he could use the power of his share-holding. But for the moment, and by the simple vote of those present, he was out of the chair of the company he had created.

"Immediately I resigned," said Reo, "they began to vote benefits for themselves. I had been one of the first people in Britain to offer incentives to the people around me but I had never expected to run into a situation like this. I had thought I had around me the most loyal people in the land."

The meeting had not been a long one but it was decidedly rowdy. At one point, Andros, who was voting with his father and Graham Lewis, was standing on a chair directing oaths at Donald Macdonald.

Reo Stakis walked out of the room saying he would sue them all personally for overturning the decision on Professor Smith. Graham Lewis stepped in to be chairman as part of a holding operation, but the following week was something of a shambles within the organisation.

For Andros Stakis it had been a crippling blow: "I was over the moon about Roland Smith coming in as chairman. I thought he would be the right man to bring me up and give a training in dealing with the City, the banks and the Press. Of course John Loughray knew that if Smith arrived his own future would not be so secure."

Andros confessed to tears at that stormy meeting. In the circumstances, his father called in Schroders, the merchant bankers, who asked the four executives to think hard about what they were doing and to come back with an answer at a meeting in their

London office two days later. Already in the picture about what had been happening, Roland Smith turned up for the showdown at Schroders to see if anything had changed. But nothing had.

He was told to his face that he was not acceptable as chairman of Stakis. The executives felt he had come in by the back door, behind their backs, and they were not prepared to work with him.

Predictably, Smith was very upset by what he heard. Among other considerations, he was losing £100,000 a year for his two-day week, plus his Jaguar and driver. The outcome of all this was that Mr Stakis was reinstated as chairman, at least for the time being, and the feeling within the company was that, if only he had chosen John Loughray, his trusted aide from the very early days, the other executives would have nursed Andros along when John retired at sixty.

With Professor Smith's appointment already announced, he had been due to take office on 1st October. The company magazine was ready and printed, with the new chairman's face all over the front cover. Donald Macdonald had to tell the public relations department that the magazine would have to be withdrawn. Why? He would tell them later. The 3000 copies were taken out of circulation and destroyed.

Reo Stakis now suspected that some of his top men were following agendas of their own. Stuart Jenkins, for example, did not endear himself by declaring that he would like to lead a management buy-out of the pubs division, of which he was the manager. "You either drop that idea or you go!" was Reo's ultimatum.

From the company's point of view, the question of a successor to Reo remained unresolved but the man himself was now as keenly aware as any that someone had to be found, preferably one who would favour Andros.

The next name to appear had a strong connection with the Stakis company stockbrokers, the old-established Glasgow firm of Speirs and Jeffrey in Renfield Street, which was owned by the family of Herbert Waddell, famous Scottish rugby internationalist of his day, and which was then run by two of his sons, Robin and Alan. But it was a third son, Gordon Waddell, another famous Scottish rugby internationalist like his father, whose name came into the frame as a possible chairman.

During an illustrious career, Waddell had been twice to South Africa with the British Lions and it was to that country that he later returned, furnished with an American business degree, to work for the well-known industrialist Harry Oppenheimer, chairman of Anglo-American among other things. He married Oppenheimer's daughter Mary and became a key figure in the family empire, remaining close to his father-in-law even after the marriage broke up.

Entering his fifties, Gordon Waddell returned to Scotland in the late 1980s and with his vast experience of international business was always going to be the target for a top job in this country. Now he was being presented as a possible chairman of Stakis.

He met the management team at the Grosvenor Hotel, where he was given a chance to "sell" himself. At the end, Frank O'Callaghan spoke for his colleagues when he said they would be happy to collaborate with Mr Waddell on one condition. They had all been with the company for most of their working lives and, since they didn't really know the man, they would like special contracts.

There is little doubt that some of them were seeing the writing on the wall and starting to think of exit routes and possible compensation. Whereas they were already on two-year contracts, O'Callaghan made it plain they now wanted three years. Waddell's response was blunt and to the point, that he would not be inclined to give them contracts at all.

Anyone working for him in the past knew that, in the event of anything going wrong, there was no cause for complaint at the parting of the ways. That had always been attended to generously and peaceably.

When Frank O'Callaghan persisted, Waddell threw up his hands in resignation and said "Mr Stakis, thank you for the offer but it is a full-time chairman this company needs and I cannot give it that amount of time."

So another candidate bit the dust, only to be followed by George Hill from Bass, who was introduced at a private dinner in the Grosvenor Hotel, Glasgow, on 19th May, 1987. As it happened, Donald Macdonald remembered him from his own days with British Transport Hotels and, because of his limited regard for the man, was held responsible for putting his colleagues against him.

30

KEY MAN RESIGNS

Matters dragged on through 1987 until Donald Macdonald took a positive step which changed the direction of the company—and raised fury in some of his executive colleagues. As boss of Hotels and Inns, the biggest division within the organisation, he was finding himself hopelessly diverted from his major responsibilities and became so sick of it all that he felt there was only one thing to do.

At a late-night meeting in the autumn of that year he told his fellow executives that, if Reo's next proposal was at all sensible, he was planning to go along with it for the sake of getting some semblance of normality back into the business. John Loughray took the bombshell with characteristic calmness but Stuart Jenkins was furious and bitter.

Frank O'Callaghan thought Macdonald had been bribed by Reo but nothing of the sort had happened. It was entirely his own decision, taken because he hoped that squabbling would be replaced by peace, though he was later to acknowledge that peace is a commodity you cannot buy.

"What was happening to the company was crazy," he later explained. "People were spending more time on all the troubles than on running the business. I had 3000 people reporting to me and just as the business was suffering, I myself was suffering."

Well, Reo Stakis's next proposal did seem reasonably acceptable. He was planning to bring in three non-executive directors,
including two knights of the realm, Sir Kenneth Alexander, well-
known economist from the academic world, and Sir Charles Fraser,
the high-profile Edinburgh lawyer with a guiding finger in many
a corporate pie. The third name was Charles Bystram, a London-
based figure from the City.

With the deeply religious background of an island upbringing,
Macdonald was impressed by Fraser's credentials. By all accounts,
here was a man of the utmost integrity, pillar of Edinburgh society,
royal purse-bearer, a leading lawyer with the prestigious firm of
W. and J. Burness and not least a son of the manse, his distinguished father, the Very Rev. Dr John A. Fraser, having been
Moderator of the General Assembly of the Church of Scotland in
1958.

Professor Alexander, too, was a man of good name and together
they would surely bring enormous credibility. Here at least, Reo
Stakis and Donald Macdonald were at one, the chairman saying
they should be extremely honoured that people of the calibre of Sir
Charles were joining the board.

At the next meeting it was indeed the vote of Macdonald, now
split from his colleagues in this respect, which swayed a decision
in Reo's favour and gave him the support of three new directors
who would be firmly within his camp. Reo took him aside afterwards and said: "I didn't expect you to do that but I will never
forget it."

"I feel quite embarrassed about it," was the reply. "But I do
realise, like the others, that my days here are numbered and I
would ask you to remember one thing. When my time comes to
leave the company, I want it to be done in a dignified way."

Reo Stakis was relieved to know he had now regained control
of his board, having reached a stage of frustration where he was
tempted to make public the fact that his senior men were making

life difficult. There had been recent publicity about Peter Tyrie having gone against his board at Bells Whisky, so delivering that company into the hands of Guinness. Such a public showdown would have been unlikely to bring much credit to the Stakis executives.

So Sir Charles Fraser bounded upon the stage, having already influenced some decisions behind the scenes. It transpired that he had been the one who persuaded Mr Stakis that he really should stand down and first suggested Gordon Waddell as chairman. It was also his idea that, in order to regain his lost control of the board, he should bring in the three new men, including himself.

Fraser soon formed the opinion that the executive directors at Stakis were sound people. Loughray, O'Callaghan, Macdonald and Jenkins were Reo's boys. He had made them what they were and had helped them towards a share-holding position in which all were very comfortable.

"But they had grown from being his boys into substantial businessmen in their own right," said Sir Charles, "and Reo had little understanding of how to manage a board, expecting that people would just do what they were told. They wanted the company to do certain things and he did not; so there was a complete impasse."

With Waddell out of the picture, Sir Charles turned his head-hunting talents towards George Mathewson, who had been running the Scottish Development Agency but was likely to be leaving that post soon. He introduced him to the chairman, found that they struck an immediate rapport and began to work out a package which could be offered to Mathewson.

Unknown to Sir Charles, however, there was something else in the offing. The former SDA boss had just four days to decide on an offer from the Royal Bank of Scotland which would lead to the post of chief executive. When he discovered this, he helped George Mathewson to make up his mind: "You go to the Royal Bank, George. I think it is more your scene."

Back at Stakis, whatever Sir Charles may have thought of the top executives, they were less impressed with him and his fellow knight, Sir Kenneth Alexander, who were seen as lapdogs brought in to smooth the way for Andros to follow his father. As one executive said: "Charles Fraser would openly praise Andros, saying what a wonderful guy he was. Naturally, Reo loved it. The rest of us knew better."

By his support of Reo in the promotion of Andros, the insider feeling was that Sir Charles failed to see the damage which was being done to the company and that he watched as the ship was buffeted.

Donald Macdonald was now regretting that he had backed the appointment of the three wise men from outside and was coming to the conclusion that, with their similar kind of peasant backgrounds, he and Reo had been naïve in believing that people of pedigree were beyond reproach. With a more street-wise upbringing in the Castlemilk housing scheme of Glasgow, Frank O'Callaghan had been more perceptive. Donald also envied Frank's ability to talk straight to people without causing offence, when offence could so easily be taken.

With Andros in the ascendancy and the long-standing relationship between his father and John Loughray now virtually at an end, the popular managing director was ready to quit. In a soured atmosphere, he felt within himself that he was not performing and that it was better to go.

So Loughray walked into the chairman's office on a January day of 1988 and tendered his resignation. By then he and the boss were hardly on speaking terms and he felt his notice was accepted without much regret. From his own point of view, it was with much sadness that he brought to an end his twenty-eight years with the Stakis organisation.

For the shipyard worker's son from Knightswood, Glasgow, it had been in many ways a spectacular career, bringing him power, position and riches he might hardly have dreamed about in those early days when he found himself hitched to the rising star of Stakis. Whatever their differences, Reo had been good to his staff and John Loughray would walk away a wealthy man. He had built up a block of 1.3 million shares which, selling at roughly a pound each, made him a millionaire before he counted the settlement arrangements.

He had long since established his wife and family in a sumptuous villa in the most exclusive part of Milngavie and knew there would be non-executive opportunities available to him, not that he was pressing for work. In the event, he became a director of the Scottish Exhibition and Conference Centre and the Scottish Tourist Board, with an involvement in the Achrannie Hotel in Arran.

Most satisfying of all, he was able to act as banker to his three children, all of whom followed him into the hotel industry. Michael and Alan have their own hotels in Pitlochry and Alloa while daughter Nicola owns the Banff Springs Hotel on the Moray Firth coast.

Casting an eye on the people he was leaving behind, Loughray knew that O'Callaghan was a clever and able man who liked to look after No 1. As for Donald Macdonald, he remembered the interview at which he engaged him, warming to the young man when he confessed that he had been fired from a previous post as assistant manager at the Royal Stuart Hotel in Glasgow. Regarded by colleagues as a workaholic, Macdonald had a genial personality which nevertheless belied a streak of steel within.

Stuart Jenkins had left the company but returned to run the casinos when they needed someone who understood not only figures but the whole control system required for the gaming business.

On Loughray's departure, dismay was the emotion which spread among executives like Tony Lang, who felt the place would fall apart without him. He seemed to embody the spirit of the company. Many looked to Frank O'Callaghan for their survival but little did they know that he was now wishing he was in a position to follow John Loughray through the door.

He claimed that, as financial director, his task of keeping Andros under control was proving well nigh impossible. He had refused, for example, to sign the cheque for David Aspin's Porsche but it was delivered nevertheless. He also felt his health was suffering and there came a stage when he was hell-bent on getting out.

31

ARISE SIR REO!

If Reo Stakis was feeling the strain of events in his beloved company there was cause for relief and rejoicing in 1988 when he was honoured with a knighthood by Mrs Thatcher's government. It was granted, not for his support of the Conservative Party but for the jobs he had provided and the boost he had given to the hotel industry of this country.

Accompanied by Annitsa and daughters Niki, Ridi and Stassia, he went to Buckingham Palace for the investiture on 2nd November, 1988. Sir Reo, as he would now be known, was full of admiration for the Queen, a lady he had met on several occasions but who spoke to one recipient after another as if she knew something about them all.

Afterwards, the Stakis family went for a meal to celebrate a wonderful day. It all seemed a far cry from that Cypriot childhood and proved once again what an unpredictable business this life really was. While filling him with pride, the knighthood itself would not affect the demeanour of Sir Reo, who was too solid a citizen for that. Indeed he would later reflect that, in practical terms, what he noticed most of all was the number of letters and requests which began to multiply!

If that day at Buckingham Palace proved a highlight in his life, relaxation from the daily stress of business would always be found in the sport of game shooting. It was something which had interested him from an early age and would become his only real hobby, albeit an expensive one.

From the Glorious Twelfth of August through to January, it would become his annual routine to invite an impressive list of friends to join him at his various shoots. He would rent the shooting at Glassingall estate, Dunblane, from Colonel Readman, an arrangement which survived until 1996.

There were other shoots at Garden of Buchlyvie and at Crawfordjohn, to which Frances Timoney would drive in the early morning of 12th August so that she could spirit the first grouse of the season back to the Pond Hotel or the Grosvenor in Glasgow in time for dinner that evening.

Even into his eighties, Sir Reo was playing host to friends like Lord Elgin, Lord Mansfield of Scone, Sir Malcolm Rifkind, Iain Bett the builder, Ian Galloway the butcher, Peter Balfour, his friend from Scottish and Newcastle days, George Abrami, the well-known surgeon, Hamish Grossart the financier, Tom and Drew Howie, David MacRobert his lawyer, and Aldo Nardini from the ice-cream family in Largs.

For the Glassingall outings, the jolly party would gather for a lavish breakfast at Dunblane Hydro, enjoy a morning's sport and return to Sir Reo's home where Lady Stakis would lay on a memorable three-course lunch.

On occasion he would be joined by fellow-hoteliers like Charles Forte, who would stay with Sir Reo at Dunblane. Latterly he was renting two days here and two days there, at places like Rossie Priory Estate, Inchture, on the road from Perth to Dundee. Nothing ever came cheap in shooting, but none of that was ever grudged by the host.

Sir Reo saw it in the light of sharing good times with friends, since he and Lady Stakis were not the kind of people to indulge in a great deal of home entertaining. Of a retiring nature, Lady Stakis was more of a charming home-maker than a social figure, keeping the domestic flag flying when her husband was fulfilling his many engagements. Indeed she would sometimes be relieved of the social round when Ridi would accompany her father.

Meanwhile, back at the business, further opportunities had arisen for Andros with the departure of John Loughray, the managing director. Sir Reo felt he should take on the title of chief executive and extolled his energy, vision and sound academic background. He was the son of a 26 per cent shareholder and founder of the company and on paper at least seemed all they could wish for.

Sir Charles Fraser felt no qualms about endorsing such an appointment, though he was soon to discover that, for all his other qualities, Andros was lacking in people skills. Board meetings, which had never been of the classical variety, suddenly became an embarrassment.

For all that, Sir Reo was reporting in his 1989 statement that "I am confident that, with our financial strength, our operating skills and enhanced management team, we are well placed to capitalise on all opportunities in the years ahead."

The group was charging on with the most ambitious expansion in its history. The hotels division was investing heavily in a chain of Country Courts, aimed at the business traveller. The Ashbourne nursing homes were expanding ambitiously, the casinos and pubs were poised to resume growth and the property division was said to be working on a variety of developments across the country.

At the age of thirty-three, Andros was into his stride, gaining initial approval from the City, which keeps an eye on the calibre and progress of senior executives. For the first two years the profits were rising as before and the new ventures seemed in good heart.

Sir Reo was proud that his elder son was at last in position and showing signs of measuring up to the task. He was not unaware that top executives still resented the boss's son and conceded that Andros was no angel, proving himself unable to get on with those around him. Andros fell out with people like O'Callaghan, Macdonald and Jenkins and was causing internal concern with the way he was buying sites and spending money.

Management bills were soaring and Scottish Business Insider was reporting that between 1988 and 1990 the number of non-board executives earning more than £40,000 went up from six to twenty-seven. Deputy managers were driving around in Jaguars and Mercedes. Costs had run out of control in the property division while its managing director, David Aspin, still enjoyed the life of a jet-setter.

On top of all that, there was a recession to wreak its havoc, with profits badly hit and property values collapsing. In the general disarray, Andros brought in a highly-paid consultant from America who was not telling them anything they did not know before. That same gent, by the name of Bill Teich, became involved in the bizarre tale of how finance director Frank O'Callaghan came to leave the company. But that would lie in the future.

32

PR ROLE FOR PAGETT

Though Reo Stakis was good with people, a friendly face not hard to like, he was well into his business career before he made serious contact with the Press. That gap was bridged on his behalf by a personable gent called Murray Thornton, who was working for a local council in Ayrshire when he encountered Mr Stakis one day. The latter was impressed by his style and invited him to become the company's public relations officer.

That role was still a developing art in the 1960s and its function had been undertaken in the early stages by a vivacious lady called Jean Cameron.

Thornton had a keen eye for what would make a story and many a journalist from that period would tell you that the first meeting with Reo Stakis came about as a result of an approach from the new PR man, who was suggesting an interesting angle. Like all good PR men, Murray Thornton knew better than to seek attention with what was no more than a free plug for the company. Journalists could be sure there was something worth pursuing.

In the case of Reo Stakis, the man's own life story was a good starting-point for a newspaperman, with its element of rags-to-riches. Murray Thornton forged many a link and left Reo Stakis with good contacts and friends in the media long after he himself had gone.

That public relations task was taken up with greater urgency in the latter part of 1988 by a former civil servant who had carved himself a notable reputation in a role which was increasingly being described as director of communications.

Alex Pagett was born at Gorebridge, near Edinburgh, and studied agriculture before turning to the information services and landing in Whitehall, making his way through Downing Street to become the chief press contact at the Scottish Office. At one stage he was working for Malcolm Rifkind, a prominent Conservative Minister of the time, and it was through that association that he moved out of the Civil Service and took over as communications director for the Tory Party in Scotland in the late 1980s.

It was a short-lived and unhappy experience which at least served to propel him more swiftly to the commercial sector. Alex Pagett was just the calibre of man now required by the Stakis organisation, which had recently run into problems with the departure of John Loughray. Taking the title of chief executive, Andros Stakis had virtually replaced the former managing director but his various qualities still left him with a major difficulty in communicating.

Pagett was seen as the man who would establish better connections, not only with the outside world but within the company, where there seemed to be a developing rift between the Stakis family and the other executives. He surveyed his new domain and deduced that those executives had one agenda and the family, supported by the non-executive directors, had another; there seemed no meeting ground for reconciliation.

Seeking to assess the situation objectively, he felt Andros had some good ideas but lacked the strategic focus to see them through to fruition, perhaps pushing too many at one time till the waters became muddied. If some of his better ideas had been supported by colleagues, matters might have been different. He did, for example, have a strategy for developing the Country Court Hotels which was well focused.

The Marriott courtyard principle was a successful formula but part of the strategy was that he would have to sell existing properties to help finance his programme. Andros had also seen the wisdom of developing the Ashbourne Homes for the elderly.

This diversification into health care was somewhat ahead of its time. The opportunity was spotted when it seemed the government would be forced to close many of the older homes which were deemed to be fire hazards. There would therefore be an opening for the more modern, up-to-date establishment though, as it happened, the government did not enforce new rules as rigidly as expected.

Stakis had twenty Ashbourne Homes all the way from Aberdeen to the south of England and there were sites for twenty-five more. But the scheme was soaking up cash and Andros found himself unable to sell the properties which would have provided the finance. Without that finance, he was heading for troubled times. Too much activity was costing too much money and none of this would be helped by the oncoming recession.

33

FRANK FALLS FOR A FOUNTAIN

That bizarre incident which would decide the future of finance director Frank O'Callaghan happened at the El Paraiso Hotel in Spain, a Stakis property between Marbella and Gibraltar which they had acquired at a price of £20,000 per room. This was deemed a bargain, with Donald Macdonald intending to turn a hundred of the two hundred rooms into fifty luxury timeshare apartments, the revenue from which would have paid for the hotel.

Frank O'Callaghan had gone out to El Paraiso for a golfing holiday with a group of Glasgow business and professional friends when his eye landed on a fountain which had been installed at the hotel. It seemed to him not only a waste of money but a poor piece of workmanship so he challenged the local management about the wisdom of such a monstrosity.

That evening, he and his party went for a night out. It was on their return to the hotel that some of his friends thought the least they could do was to put poor old Frank out of his misery. A few libations had undoubtedly been taken but, in the name of direct action, they jumped into the water and smashed up the offending fountain. Completely demolished it!

Now, by cruel coincidence, the startled onlookers included none other than the American Bill Teich, who happened to be there on holiday with his wife. The matter was reported on the phone to Sir Reo—and that was what brought matters to a head as far as Frank O'Callaghan was concerned. When he arrived back in Glasgow he was promptly sacked.

Sir Reo told him: "You are not happy. I am not happy. Perhaps it is better that we call it a day." He personally handed him his letter of dismissal and O'Callaghan walked out of the West Regent Street headquarters for ever. Years later, though dismissal was what he had really been dreaming about, he still regarded it as a sad and sorry affair which caused him much regret.

Some time later, O'Callaghan's brother died at the age of forty-six and one of the most touching letters came from Sir Reo. "That pleased me no end," he said. "I wrote back and said how much I appreciated his gesture and hoped that we would meet again one day."

When Sir Reo went to break the news that O'Callaghan had just been sacked, Donald Macdonald told him they were living in crazy times and that he would appreciate it if the chairman would put together a package so that he too could depart. But Sir Reo had no wish for his hotel boss to go and assured him that he was totally secure.

Son Andros held no such high opinions of Macdonald, feeling he was not the man to take the company forward to its next phase. He said: "I should have got rid of him earlier. He and I did not share the same aspirations. My view of the hotel business was that you needed a brand image which had a relationship, as with Ken McCulloch who founded One Devonshire Gardens and the Malmaison chain, where you knew there was a specific standard of decor, quality and service."

At one point Andros told Macdonald to his face: "You have been too long with the company and you would be better away. I have someone else to do your job." That someone was Udo Schlentrich, former manager of the London Dorchester who had also worked in America. But Andros was soon ready to admit that he had made the wrong choice.

Not yet sacked, however, Macdonald went off to Cornwall on 3rd April 1989 to look over a timeshare complex they were considering when, unknown to him, Andros turned up at the hotels headquarters in East Kilbride, intending to deliver a rallying call to the troops who were answerable to Macdonald.

Instead, he came under fire from senior staff who demanded to know what was going on. He revealed that he was going to get rid of Macdonald—but he had not yet told him so. He had already approached Gerry Smith, who worked closely with Macdonald in the hotels division, and said: "If Donald leaves, will you promise to stay?" A Jaguar and a 30 per cent pay rise were in the offer but Smith turned it down.

All this was happening in the lead-up to Andros's wedding, which took place at Glasgow University Chapel on the first Sunday of April and thereafter at the company's Normandy Hotel at Renfrew. He was marrying Barbara McMahon, a popular columnist on the Glasgow *Evening Times*, and Macdonald and his wife were among the invited guests. The selectivity of that guest-list created its own ripples, people like Gerry Smith and Tony Lang being excluded.

On his return from honeymoon at the end of April, Andros attended a board meeting and was said to have been more civil to people than ever before. Marriage seemed to be working its own wonders. Donald Macdonald took the opportunity to clarify his own departure date and severance conditions but Andros was now inclined to backtrack.

When he had reported to Sir Reo that he was sacking Macdonald, there was said to have been "a real rammy" between father and son. But the die was cast and Macdonald was holding him to his decision. Much as he liked Macdonald, Sir Reo felt he had not been making an effort to work with Andros and pursued a suspicion that he may have been planning a future of his own outwith Stakis.

Macdonald secured his package and left the company on 25th May 1989, appreciating the generosity of a deal which gave him six months of money for doing nothing, a further two years of pay and a bonus for eighteen months of discreet silence. On top of all that, he walked out with £900,000 worth of shares, of which he cashed £300,000 worth to finance his own business venture.

The lad from Harris had done not too badly for himself. Before leaving Stakis, he knew that Andros wanted to sell a number of hotels and offered to buy five or six of them as part of his departing deal. To that end, he lined up funding of £90 million but Sir Reo put his foot down on the proposition.

At least Macdonald now knew he could raise the finance and it was just a matter of awaiting the right opportunity. In Aberdeen one day he called at the offices of Abtrust, the highly successful finance company, to see Calum McLeod, another man from the Isles. They were joined by a second Abtrust man who suggested that Macdonald should make a bid for two north-east hotels currently on the market, the Waterside at Peterhead and the prestigious Ardoe House on the edge of Aberdeen.

He studied the proposition, borrowed several millions from the Bank of Scotland, put together a bid for the two Aberdeenshire hotels and launched himself into business at a most opportune moment. In the early spring of 1990 the outbreak of the Gulf War sent oil prices rocketing and what had been a good business in the oil-rich north-east of Scotland was suddenly a dramatically better one.

By the following May, Macdonald was buying Inchyra House at Polmont in central Scotland and beginning to establish a chain of hostelries in that country-house mould. The company was also taking on the management of Barratt timeshare properties, with an agreement to buy 50 per cent of them, and gaining favour with a grateful Bank of Scotland by successfully managing and turning into profit a long list of hotels which had landed in their lap, having come unstuck in the recession.

For all of this, Macdonald had the assistance of some tried and trusted friends from his days at Stakis. Gerry Smith had become his operations director, Jim Busby his finance director and the non-executive chairman was none other than Frank O'Callaghan.

An English businessman, Trevor Hemming, whose personal fortune was estimated at £300 million, became a major financial backer and Macdonald Hotels were now a force to be reckoned with in the industry. By the late 1990s they owned twenty-four hotels, from Peterhead to Botley Park at Southampton, and were managing thirty-three others.

When the company reached the Stock Exchange in 1996, Donald Macdonald himself became worth an immediate £20 million and even Gerry Smith could claim to be a millionaire ten times over. Frank O'Callaghan had invested a mere £50,000 but soon found himself richer by between four and five million. The casualties of troubled times at Stakis had done very well for themselves. Young Andros was not joking when he said: "I did Macdonald the greatest favour of his life when I sacked him!"

Looking back more in sorrow than gloating, Donald Macdonald laid a large share of the blame for those troubles at the door of the non-executive directors at Stakis. He regarded their contribution as weak and superficial—he was particularly disappointed in Sir Charles Fraser—and thought if they had been of the calibre which he himself acquired in his own business, the Stakis shares would have been standing at a very much higher figure. Instead, the price of 130p in the mid-1980s had dropped to under 30p and regained that former price only in 1998.

34

TIME FOR ACTION

To whatever extent the Stakis troubles could be blamed on the conflict between top executives and Sir Reo's own son and intended successor, it could be said that he had paid a dear price in losing such high-calibre management for the sake of love and loyalty to his own blood.

In seeking to promote his elder son, he took the view that Andros was a bright and well-educated young man, energetic and ambitious, who should be allowed to be his own person, without being hampered by the shadow of a successful father. With the benefit of hindsight, however, he frankly acknowledged that he had made a big mistake in bringing Andros into the company at such an early age.

"I should have let him go to work somewhere else for ten years or so before coming back to join me," he said. "And then I should have kept an eye on him after that. By not doing all that, I made my biggest mistake. It cost the company and all of us an awful lot."

For all his family loyalty and his feeling that the established executives made life difficult for Andros, Sir Reo never shirked the fact that his son had an unfortunate knack of falling out with people and that the brashness of his youth could so easily be interpreted as arrogance.

*　　　*　　　*

In the ups and downs of his business life, Reo would tell stories of deals that succeeded and opportunities that slipped away. The story of what became known as the Thistle Hotels was a case in point. He had a call one day from a friend who thought Reo should make a bid for the group, which was on offer from Lord Delfont's EMI company at an asking price of £27 million.

Reo was keen on the idea and had the prospects checked out, but his advisers felt some of the leases were not good. In deciding to pass up the opportunity, however, he chose to alert his friend Peter Balfour, chairman of Scottish and Newcastle, the brewers with whom he had done so much business.

"They are having a board meeting at EMI right now so you should phone Lord Delfont very soon," he advised.

Reo having cleared the way by assuring him that Stakis would not be interested in such a sale, Balfour did indeed put through a call to Delfont but found the well-known theatrical figure in less than co-operative mood. Yes, they might be interested in selling but he was just leaving for the Cannes Film Festival.

"Well, I could come to Cannes and discuss it there," said Peter Balfour, seeking to hold the advantage of his early warning. He and his financial director boarded a plane and headed for the Riviera, catching up with Lord Delfont at his private apartment and meeting his gorgeous wife, who was a former Miss England.

Considering the little gestures which sometimes turn a deal, Balfour rushed out and returned with a gush of roses for Lady Delfont. Her husband said they had to go for lunch with some of the stars who were in town for the festival but the Scottish visitors were welcome to stay in the apartment and read the papers.

"What shall I do if the phone rings?" Peter Balfour asked.

"Just say you are the butler," Delfont suggested as he disappeared.

Needless to say, the phone did ring and the chairman of Scottish and Newcastle played out the part of butler to perfection before entering into negotiations which ended with him buying the EMI hotels for the asking price of £27 million. That deal became the basis of the Thistle Hotels, stretching northward from the Tower Hotel by the Thames in London.

A few years later, after Peter Balfour had retired, Reo Stakis was invited to a wonderful lunch at the Holyrood headquarters of Scottish and Newcastle in Edinburgh. What was this all about? Well, the new boss of S&N, Alick Rankin, was presenting him with a pair of silver pheasants as a small token of their gratitude for helping them secure those hotels from Lord Delfont.

Actually, they had now sold on the Thistle Group and that purchase which had cost them £27 million represented a sizeable part of the property that had now brought back a selling price of £670 million! Reo Stakis graciously acknowledged the gesture and went off home with his silver pheasants, which were given pride of place in his lounge, still wondering what a profit of that kind might have done for the fortunes of his own company if he had decided to buy those Delfont hotels himself.

There was a postscript to that story in 1998 when Thistle Hotels were on the market once more and the Stakis organisation showed an interest in buying them. Thistle was now capitalised at £1340 million and the asking price was nearer £1800 million. However, the Glasgow company withdrew its interest.

With three of the Big Four executives now gone, Stuart Jenkins was the sole survivor, running the leisure division, which had bought the Firkin chain of pubs and was pursuing the acquisition of the Barracuda Club in Baker Street, London, which was in the hands of the Receiver.

By now, however, he was more in a mood to follow his colleagues who had left the company and even made a proposition to Sir Reo about buying out the leisure division. "There was a rumour that I was involved in a clandestine activity," he said later. "But I don't know what I was supposed to have done."

Matters soon came to a head. When the three senior men in Jenkins' department found themselves in disagreement with Andros one day, they promptly stalked out of the room. Just as promptly, Andros decided they were going to be sacked.

A statement of dismissal was prepared and Stuart Jenkins found himself under instructions to read it to the men concerned—in the presence of Andros. The men were aghast at what had happened and looked towards Jenkins for some explanation or support. Little did they know what would happen next.

Once Jenkins had gone through the motions of sacking his men, Andros told him that he too was sacked, demanding that he be off the premises by 5pm. Andros said: "I felt let down by Stuart Jenkins. I had given him more opportunities than the others. He had an established business and he had to acquire twenty or thirty pubs but in my short time he didn't buy any."

The three sacked men then realised that Jenkins had been no more than the messenger of their misfortune and bore him no grudge. In fact, within a short time they were all business colleagues again.

As the last of the main casualties, Jenkins drew up a business plan of his own and Scottish Brewers said they would give him support if he could pull it all together. Fresh from their sacking, Bill Morrison became his operations director and Bill Hamilton the finance director, while John McNulty was in charge of development in a company they called Eagle Taverns.

Up and running by June 1991, they began to pursue businesses they knew were for sale. They launched themselves with seven pubs, including Shenanigans in Sauchiehall Street, Glasgow, and by 1997 had built up that number to forty-four, with a turnover of £20 million. The acquisitions now ranged from the Waverley Hotel in Peterhead, Ferryhill House in Aberdeen and the Torrance in

East Kilbride to the Halt Bar and Queen's Cross Bar in Glasgow, Jock Tamson's in Kilmarnock, the Cellar in Paisley and the Old Govan Arms and Whistler's Mother back in Glasgow.

But nothing is for ever. The ambitious plans of the former Stakis men, which might have led to the Stock Exchange, did not materialise before they were overtaken by events. The venture capital organisation known as 3i became the majority shareholder, and by 1999 both Stuart Jenkins and Bill Hamilton had left the company. Sadly, John McNulty died, and Bill Morrison became the sole survivor of the original team, agreeing to remain until his planned retirement date later in the year.

Before embarking on his Eagle Taverns venture, Stuart Jenkins was being tipped for a prominent post in a totally different sphere— the chief executive's job at Celtic Football Club. In the approaching era of Fergus McCann, the multi-millionaire who came back from Canada to salvage the club with his own money before running into massive controversy, that would have presented a rather different challenge. He chose to turn away from that tempting situation, however, and set himself a goal of another sort. (Intriguingly, in 1999 his old Stakis colleague Frank O'Callaghan was invited to take over as non-executive chairman of Celtic, on the departure of Mr McCann.)

Like Macdonald, Stuart Jenkins blamed much of the Stakis trouble on the non-executives. "They were out of touch with what was happening," he said. "They didn't spend time with the executives to see where the problems really lay and were too concerned with appeasing Sir Reo. If they had seen Andros they would have seen the problem. But they were a million miles away from the issues."

Initially it had been the executive directors who had doubts about Andros, but Sir Charles Fraser was later to concede that they had been right and the rest of the board, including himself, had been wrong in their judgement.

Having admitted that much, however, Sir Charles went on to

maintain that, unwittingly, it had all turned out for the best as far as the company was concerned. "We went through a dreadful period in which the Stock Market had turned downwards, the recession was biting, hotel occupancy was poor and we were really struggling."

Debts were mounting and the consensus view in financial circles was that they were largely due to the expansion strategy of Andros Stakis in his role of chief executive. With the enthusiasm of youth, and not a little forward thinking, Andros had embarked on those ambitious schemes at the Ashbourne Homes, the Country Court Hotels, the fifty-strong pub division, including the Firkin chain, and the group's property expansion.

All this was eating into the earnings just as the markets were turning sour. Financial analysts said the strategy was wrong and left no defence against that double nightmare of recession and property slump. Debts had already risen beyond £200 million and were likely to reach £240 million within three months.

Sir Reo was clinging to the hope that they could raise an extra £100 million and that, given those three months, his son could become an important figure in the City. But time was running out and by then the banks were beginning to raise the alarm about the level of debt.

Aware that matters were coming to a head at that stage in 1990, Sir Charles Fraser decided that Sir Reo had to be confronted with the facts. It would not be an easy task, nor would it be well received. But it had to be done and the man to do it, since communication was his business, would be Alex Pagett, who had the knack of talking honestly while employing enough tact to soften the blow. Having taken the initiative and been responsible for setting up the meeting, Sir Charles was full of admiration for the way Pagett conducted himself.

The moment arrived with a phone-call, summoning him to Sir Reo's office in West Regent Street. He didn't have much warning.

Sir Charles, who was already in the room with Sir Reo, motioned him to say his piece, clearing the way with "There will be no recriminations."

So Alex Pagett had to deliver the general opinion that Andros was not doing his job. As the communications boss, he himself had problems on his hands and it would do no-one any favours to disguise them. For a start, he had soon discovered that the Stock Market felt Andros was short on credibility. It did not believe he had the capacity for his onerous task and therefore had no faith in the company as a future investment.

"Sir Reo was far from happy with me!" was Pagett's understatement. The boss certainly did not take kindly to the approach, feeling this was not what he had expected from his PR man. Indeed it took some time before better relations were restored.

Faced with some blunt facts, however, Sir Reo now realised that something had to be done and it was at this point that Sir Charles Fraser suggested the move which would alter the entire course of the Stakis organisation. There was one man, he felt, who could save this company, a name which had cropped up at the same time as George Mathewson and Gordon Waddell but was now more urgently needed than ever.

He had preceded Mathewson as boss of the Scottish Development Agency and it was his particular brand of toughness, as much as his salvaging abilities, which were now required at Stakis. This man, who had gained a nationwide reputation as a "company doctor," was Sir Lewis Robertson.

35

ENTER THE COMPANY DOCTOR

For Sir Lewis Robertson, it all began with a phone-call from Sir Charles Fraser, who was already well-known to him not only as a leading Edinburgh lawyer but as a kind of people broker when it came to business affairs. The financial community of the Scottish capital is sufficiently compact for everyone to have a good working knowledge of everyone else.

As a member of the Stakis board, Sir Charles had suggested his name and now he was seeking a meeting between Sir Lewis and Sir Reo, in the hope that the former might be willing to take over as chairman of the company.

Outwith business circles, Sir Lewis Robertson was some vague and lofty figure, not much known to the general public except for that journalistic label of "company doctor." So who was he?

Lewis Robertson grew up in a well-known Dundee family which was in the jute and textile industry. Leaving Trinity College, Glenalmond, in 1939 he started in accountancy just before the war and, without completing the course, went straight into the family business. His war service of unravelling enemy codes no doubt stood him in good stead when it came to probing and solving the problems of business in the years ahead.

His brother having been killed in that war, Lewis was at the forefront of his own family enterprise in 1965 when it merged with a larger family business to become Scott and Robertson, of which he first became managing director and later chairman. According to Sir Lewis, the Scott family members did not like what he was showing them about the 20th century and, pulling together their superior voting power, they were ready to oust him from the company.

Saving them the trouble, in what he colourfully described as "the revolt of the pygmies," he resigned in 1970 and lived to thank them for kick-starting his career in so many other directions, when he might well have spent the rest of his life within the limits of Dundee. In 1971 he became chief executive of Grampian Holdings, a well-known Scottish name, and embarked on what was his first attempt at rescuing a company in difficulties.

Five years later, he was approached with the offer of becoming the first chief executive of the new Scottish Development Agency. After five more years he was back in the hurly-burly of sorting out business, gaining that reputation of the "company doctor," who was on call to examine the ailing body, diagnose the problem and restore it to good health.

Among the companies seeking his help were Havelock Europa, one of the United Kingdom's largest shop-fitting manufacturers, and Scotland's own FJC Lilley, the construction company which undertook contracts around the world from its base in Glasgow.

Of course not everyone was enamoured of those rescue operations. While he may have brought Lilley's back from the dead, it was not hard to find thousands of small investors who would say they were among the real people who enabled that once-prosperous Scottish company to resume operations. They were the ones who had been forced to forfeit the hard-earned savings which they had patriotically invested in a Scots enterprise, only to see them vanish for ever.

Be that as it may, Sir Lewis was now being called upon to save another leading Scottish company from the brink of disaster. Sir

Reo kept the appointment at the Robertson home in Saxe Coburg Place, Edinburgh, a sedate cul-de-sac in the Stockbridge district of the capital, where Sir Lewis could count among his neighbours top men in the legal and banking professions, including George Mathewson, now chief executive of the Royal Bank, who lived three doors away.

Sir Reo climbed to the top-floor den where Sir Lewis surrounded himself not only with the books and documents you might expect but also with the full array of computer technology in which, for a man of such large and conventional status—and not in the first flush of youth—he was remarkably nimble and conversant.

Sir Lewis found his visitor to be exceedingly courteous and polite in handling what was a difficult and disturbing situation. He made it plain from the outset that, if he were to assume the role of chairman at Stakis, he must be free to take whatever measures he felt necessary for the welfare of the business.

To that end, he would require to be given proxy over the family shares. This, of course, was largely symbolic, intended to make the point that as long as he was there, he and no-one else was in charge.

Sir Reo knew well that the new chairman would inevitably form an opinion about Andros, whose performance as chief executive was not unknown to him. However, Sir Lewis would not arrive with an agenda for removing Andros, but would instead allow time to see whether, with his guidance, he thought the young man could be trained in the disciplines required.

The Royal Bank of Scotland, in the person of his neighbour, George Mathewson, was anxious that he should take on the Stakis responsibility since bankers always felt happier about lending levels when a man of proven record was in charge. Never one to hide his light, despite a peculiar shyness, Sir Lewis was not inclined to disagree that he was just the man for the job. Indeed he made it plain that he thought there was no-one else in Scotland who could fit the task so well.

By the time he arrived in 1991, the principal lieutenants, Frank O'Callaghan, Donald Macdonald and Stuart Jenkins had already been fired and John Loughray had gone of his own volition.

But if Sir Lewis had had no personal experience of the four principals, he sensed that, for all their worth, collectively they may have been there too long. He put that down to the keen sense of loyalty which Sir Reo had shown to his employees. He heard the stories of how Andros had broken up the old guard, using a fairly blunt instrument for the execution, but felt privately that what Andros had done would probably have had to be done in any case.

Whatever pruning remained as part of the restoration, he had at least been spared that part of it. This left the future of Andros himself to be considered and he was not long in coming to the conclusion that Sir Reo's son was the one around whom the main problem revolved: "He had great energy and a lot of imagination but not much self-regulation," was how Sir Lewis summed it up. "He was going too fast in certain directions, especially in spending money on the nursing homes venture and on new hotels before the availability of the necessary money had been established. By the time I got there the company was in a fairly serious financial position."

For a start, there were no fewer than twenty-one banks lending the money, most of them unaware of the existence of the others. Sir Lewis had long since discovered that too many banks were a remarkably reliable indicator of impending trouble in a company. The very fact of his arrival alerted them to the seriousness of the problem and sparked off a bout of consternation within their ranks. Indeed much of his early work was an attempt to keep the banks on side. But there was much less time available than he had thought.

He said: "The actual cash position was worsening and, while I did give as much attention as possible to the Andros situation, it was apparent we didn't have that much time to play with. In any case, it seemed doubtful if he could adapt—and I had no alternative but to reach the decision that Andros must go."

Preparing himself carefully, he broke the news to Sir Reo, telling him what he was about to do, before discussing it with the board and then calling for Andros himself. For all his inclination to react fiercely to situations, with little facility for tact, Andros nevertheless took the news calmly and correctly in Sir Lewis's view.

Sir Reo had no alternative but to accept the decision; and he did so with grace, even though he thought he had an undertaking that his son would remain in the position. If Andros took his sacking stoically, he was suffering inner devastation and withdrew to lick his wounds and consider where he had gone wrong in life. There would come a time for assessing the situation more closely and airing his opinions.

In the meantime, however, he could do little but watch as Sir Lewis Robertson, his executioner, buckled down to sorting out the problems at Stakis, the first task being to find a highly professional and skilled manager to take on the duties of chief executive.

The Stakis dynasty was coming to an end. Or rather, as Sir Lewis saw it, there were horses for courses and, for all his intelligence and imagination, Andros was not the horse for that course at that particular time.

So Andros bowed out of his father's creation with as much dignity as possible, while privately raging at what Lewis Robertson had just done. He told friends that Robertson had intimidated him, virtually saying if he didn't do as he was told he would lose his job.

"When Robertson sacked me I felt he wanted to show that he was ending the Stakis dynasty. And I will never forgive him," he declared. It was not just what had happened to him personally that rankled. There was the question of a deal which was all but signed and sealed with Scottish and Newcastle for the sale of the

Stakis pubs. Sir Lewis told him not to proceed with that deal until he had time to carry out a "strategic review."

Said Andros: "I had shaken hands on the deal, which was going to bring us a profit of £12 million. Instead, he stopped the deal, spent £500,000 on his review and then said that, having analysed the business, the decision was to sell the casinos. I said to Dad 'What is this man doing? He wants to sell the one thing you cannot sell.' "

To that extent, Andros was right. Sir Lewis later conceded that he had put a stop to Andros's deal with Scottish and Newcastle, and that he did complete the deal at a later stage—but at a greatly reduced price.

"I thought the casinos were the part to sell," he admitted, though Andros had explained why there would be no buyer. Sir Lewis came to realise that, because some London clubs had landed in trouble, no investor at that time would touch casinos with a barge-pole for fear of inheriting the problems.

In the six months leading up to Andros's departure, he had borrowed fairly extensively for the purpose of acquiring more shares to increase the family holding to 29.9 per cent, in the hope that they could retain control. Because of the way the share-price had gone, that simply added to the family's problems and put them very close to bankruptcy.

Sir Charles Fraser marvelled at how Sir Reo coped with such a devastating crisis, retaining his judgement and keeping an even keel in his dealings with people at a time when he was worth virtually nothing.

"This was a measure of his greatness," he said. "If he had not been the great wee man he was, the banks would promptly have liquidated him."

Now that the Stakis name had been sidelined from what had once been their own family company, Sir Reo put on a brave face and said that, while there was certainly a sense of humiliation, he had no sense of failure. "Very few people know what you go through in a situation like that," he said. "My main concern was that people within the company would not lose money."

Sir Reo was the first to acknowledge that Sir Lewis Robertson had a presence which was instantly recognisable. He was a large-framed man who could command a board—a solid Dundonian who had known what it was to be ousted from his own family company.

But Sir Reo's admiration for the man was limited. He was later to say: "He is without doubt one of the most egotistical men I have known in my whole life. As for the company, he did not do anything as a 'doctor'. In fact he lost us money by preventing Andros from completing that deal."

If Sir Reo was polite, there were moments of disagreement when the two men met, but not without a touch of humour. When crossing swords about Sir Reo's own terms and arrangements, Sir Lewis looked at him sternly and said: "You are trying to take advantage of a young man!" With one approaching seventy and the other eighty, Sir Reo appreciated the joke.

Working out his strategy, wisely or otherwise, Sir Lewis was quickly evaluating the people around him, deciding who to keep and who to lose, and assessing which parts of the business to hold and develop and which parts to cast off, so that money could be brought in to keep Stakis alive.

Corporate rescue, he knew, was little different from one company to another. There were set principles which had to be applied no matter where you were, and Stakis was no different. Sir Lewis was confident enough to say: "I have almost unique experience in this field and I am clever enough to see a company's problems. When I concluded that I would have to replace Andros, I sent for my most thinking head-hunter."

That man drew up two lists of candidates, one with hotel experience and the other from a plc background. Sir Lewis was going off to his holiday home outside Bordeaux and it was there he interviewed the short leet of candidates and made what he knew to be a crucial choice.

36

THE NEW BROOM

The prime target for the role of chief executive came to be David Michels, managing director of Hilton UK, who confessed that he knew very little about Stakis, beyond the fact that it was a smallish but respected competitor. It had certainly never come into the reckoning of his personal ambitions.

But the gods were working for Sir Lewis because Michels did have an ambition to be a chief executive and there was one missing part in the jigsaw of his own career. For all his knowledge of hotel operation, he had no experience of the City and its workings. If he could master this side of it, his reputation would soar.

At the interview he was perfectly frank about his deficiency but Sir Lewis was more than willing to guide him through that particular jungle. What is more, as a long-standing poker player, well practised in that game of bluff and skill, Michels knew there was an irresistible element of gamble in the Stakis job. Sir Lewis did not take long to persuade him towards a deal.

There is little doubt, as proved by subsequent events, that the most significant single achievement of Sir Lewis's stewardship was to find and appoint David Michels as chief executive of Stakis plc. They were very different animals but they complemented each other well—Michels the sound Cockney hotelier; Robertson the older-style business Scot who was a mixture of the shy and the pompous.

Historian Sir Kenneth Clark once asked the question: "What do I believe?" Answer: "Not much. But I do believe that order is better than chaos." Sir Lewis established that order at Stakis but he would rely on David Michels for his professional skills as a hotel man. Together they would dovetail into an excellent relationship.

It was part of the deal that Sir Lewis would be the teacher and for the next two years David Michels was the willing pupil. Sir Lewis, on the other hand, had a limited interest in business. The City and finance were his favourite spheres.

So who was the new man at the helm of the Stakis organisation? David Michels was brought up in the Willesden district of north London, son of a local restaurant owner who was comfortable enough to take his family on holidays abroad in the 1950s. That was when young David acquired a taste not only for travel but for hotels, which were an extension of the family interest.

After his basic education he studied at the hotel school at Hendon before joining Grand Metropolitan in the financial control department of the London Mostyn at a wage of £17 a week. He moved to the Royal Manhattan in New York and had become worldwide sales and marketing director before joining Ladbroke Hotels back in Britain.

When Ladbroke took over Hilton International in 1988, Michels cut 600 of the company's sales force across the world, many of whom were returned to hotel operation. Such improved efficiency helped to set profits soaring—and the practice of trimming unnecessary staff was something he had not forgotten when he took over at Stakis in 1991.

The inherited situation showed that the company was not quite bankrupt but it was stuck in the mire of those twenty-one banks and seemed to be getting nowhere. If stalemate had continued, the banks would probably have sold off the assets and realised just about enough to clear the debts.

So how did Michels go about the task of putting the Stakis organisation back on its feet?

Setting out to raise the morale of the company, he found that that was easier than he had anticipated. For all the problems, he soon realised Sir Reo had left such a residue of friendliness and "Stakis feeling" about the place that there was a good foundation on which to build.

In that period of the late 1980s and early 1990s when the company was heading for trouble, Sir Reo's departing executives were being replaced by a new breed of management. It was that replacement breed who were now being removed, sometimes not even to be replaced. "There were people who did not have value," was Michels' blunt comment.

Next, he decided to keep the hotels and casinos and sell off the nursing homes, the property company, the pubs and some of the other peripheral restaurants and businesses. They had to reconstruct the core business and raise money.

Whereas there had once been five divisions of the organisation operating in five different places, they had all been brought together under one roof at Atlantic Quay, by the Broomielaw in Glasgow. Michels then applied himself to the disposal of assets, £200 million of them, taking whatever prices he could get.

Two weeks after he started, there was an experience he would never forget. It was his first meeting with that array of banks, all of which had a vested interest in what had been happening at Stakis and, more importantly, what was going to happen in the future. This was foreign ground to Michels.

The Royal Bank of Scotland was prominent in the line-up but of course it was by no means alone. Facing Michels across a large table were no fewer than fifty-four people, there to look after the interests of twenty-two banks in all. The first item which rather threw him was the half-hour spent on deciding whether or not there would be smoking in the chamber.

Whether they puffed or pontificated, he was more interested in getting on with the business in hand. When the meeting finally started, this battery of financial wizards wanted to know what the new chief executive was planning for the recovery of Stakis plc. How, for example, was he going to improve the gearing?

The gearing? Michels rather upset the even tenor of events by saying he would first have to understand the terminology. What was gearing? He was not yet acquainted with the language. The bankers couldn't fathom this fellow. Was he being serious? Did he really not understand the word gearing (the ratio of a company's debt to its equity capital) or was he just testing them for reaction?

From the quizzical looks exchanged, it would have to be deduced that they were suspicious of his ignorance; which only showed how little they knew about how little he knew! Whatever the gaps in his knowledge, David Michels proved a fast learner, with Sir Lewis always on hand to unravel a mystery.

Michels began to lay down figures of what he planned to produce from the operation of the hotels and the casinos. They were impressive figures but the banks didn't believe he could do it.

So he had to show that he was prepared to put his reputation where his mouth was. If he did deliver the results as he said, would they support him? Well, yes they would. The short version of the story is that he was as good as his word—and the banks were as good as theirs.

He knew the casinos were performing reasonably well and, with his vast experience of hotels, he was confident of producing the results in that department. Occupancy levels had to be raised and margins increased; but the banks would have to allow them to invest physically in those hotels.

In only his second week in the job, he called in the manager of every hotel, casino and other unit in the group and redefined his budget and his target. One year later, those targets had been reached.

Concurrently, Michels was pursuing three other objectives which would bring the first real step towards recovery. He arranged a rights issue for £27 million, he sold the nursing homes division for £50 million and reduced the number of banks they were dealing with from twenty-two to ten.

The City sat up and took notice, realising that here were people who could deliver reliable profits in a recession, when not too many people were doing that. He then battled his way towards a mere four banks and raised £67 million with another rights issue. Now it was time to think about buying more hotels. Everyone was deep in recession, prices were down and Michels moved in to buy other people's problems, which could be turned to the Stakis advantage. By 1993 the company was beginning to be fairly prosperous.

Straddling the two managements, Alex Pagett had struggled to establish better relations with both the City and the media. He knew that the business was fundamentally sound and had merely lost its way. As it tried to re-focus itself, his role would be that of linchpin, keeping the City fully informed and making it plain that the lessons from troubled times had been learned to advantage, that there was a clear idea of where they were going and that costs were being kept under control.

Those channels of communication had to be maintained with local and national government, as well as the City, and not least with the 13,000 employees who had every right to know how their livelihood was being affected.

Pagett's role was important enough for him to be put on the executive committee of the company, a body of eight top men who dealt with the strategic direction.

David Michels did not concern himself too deeply with how the organisation had landed in a predicament. He felt the main reason had been internal politics, which was never helpful to a company. At the grass roots, he felt they had still been making money.

When he arrived, Sir Reo was already Life President and had not been involved in running the company for some time. "Everyone felt Andros was responsible but it was not just as simple as that," Michels explained. "It was a process of which Andros was only a part. You have to be cut out for a job and I reckon Einstein couldn't have run the Stakis organisation. You need qualities other than intellect and imagination. You need to be able to lead and listen and hire sensible people; you need to take advice and you need to be consistent. Above all, you need to be a businessman."

As for the Andros situation, he said: "People inheriting a business from a father tend to suffer from one of two things. They have either an inferiority complex, believing they are not as good as the father, or they have a superiority complex, determined to be twice as good as the father. I believe Andros came into the second category. The truth is that sons should not inherit companies from their fathers. It hardly ever works."

And how did Sir Reo react to the new broom? Michels continued: "He has been amazing. When you consider that I was replacing his son—and he couldn't have been madly keen on that—he has been supportive of me from the very first day. We got on well together from the first minute of our meeting."

Of course Sir Reo was still a major shareholder whose personal circumstances would depend a great deal on how well Michels performed. But there was an affinity between the two men. Michels remembered an early conversation in which Sir Reo had said: "Do you know David, not so long ago I was worth £100 million. Today I am worth nothing."

As Michels set out to rectify that situation, he said "It was not the money that mattered to Sir Reo. It was what it represented in terms of what he had achieved in life—and what he had lost."

As for the performance of Stakis, there had been a certain

advantage in getting into trouble before the recession of the early nineties and getting out of it before that recession ended. Picking up on the solid standards which had been left by the founder, he discovered that the hotels and casinos were in good order.

Now he was buying another twenty-one hotels and six or seven casinos at the relatively good prices available in the recession. So he came out of that troubled time with good stock and proceeded to build upon it. The strategy was working.

Many companies complain that, no matter how well they perform, their efforts are seldom reflected in the share price, but David Michels brushes aside such complaints and believes that, if you keep producing the results, your share price will eventually catch up. When he arrived in 1991, the Stakis shares stood at 24 pence, on a market capitalisation of £72 million. By 1998, the shares had risen to 130 pence and the capitalisation to one billion. At that stage, Michels said: "There is more in front of us than behind us."

Towards the new millennium, the portfolio of 52 hotels included the London flagship, the Metropole, bought from Lonrho in November 1996 and expanding to become the biggest hotel and conference centre in Europe. It had the advantage of standing at the Paddington terminus of the new fast-rail link to Heathrow Airport.

In another interesting development in the capital, Stakis sold its leasehold on the prestigious St Ermin's, near Westminster, but continued to run it. David Michels believed you could not own all your properties these days and that this was a means of releasing cash, maintaining a stake in hotels which belonged to other people.

On a personal level, when he took the Stakis job he regarded it as a stepping-stone in his career. After all, he had started in his native London area, worked around the world and returned to the metropolis. A move to Scotland seemed like just one more step on the way to greater things.

With his success at Stakis, however, his attitude came to be one of greater custodianship. Despite other personal offers, he became more and more focused on what he regarded as a main ambition. Envisaging it as a much larger company, he was dreaming of the day when he would take it to the Footsie 100, one of the top companies in the United Kingdom, as recorded in the *Financial Times*.

In 1998, Stakis stood at 188th position in the UK in terms of market capitalisation. To gain some perspective, Granada, which had swallowed up the Forte organisation, was eight times that size.

"But you cannot stand still," he said. "All you need to do is decide at what pace you will expand—and for what reasons. For a start, shareholders want growth. If you are employing ambitious, imaginative people, they will leave you if you don't grow. You also want to be going at the opposition. And on top of all that, it's fun to grow!"

He was surrounding himself with key people who would assist in that expansion. Neil Chisman was already in place as finance director when he arrived but there were two important appointments to secure.

For the post of managing director of the hotels he engaged Anthony Harris, formerly director of operation with the Sheraton/Ciga group. (He became yet another of Sir Lewis Robertson's neighbours in that secluded Edinburgh street!) And in 1997 the task of running the casinos went to Ian Payne, who was previously with Bass Leisure, while the chain of LivingWell health clubs would be run by Stuart Broster.

The ubiquitous Sir Charles Fraser was still there as a non-executive director, to be joined by Ian Bankier, group managing director of Burn Stewart Distillers.

When he took the Stakis job, it perhaps tells of the precarious nature of the company that Michels did not consider it wise to uproot his family from London to settle in Glasgow. By the time he immersed himself in the problems and came up with solutions, he had established a routine of life which enabled him to retain his southern home. Claiming that he needed to be in London for part of his time anyway, he simply commuted to Glasgow for two or three days a week, becoming one of the Shuttle's best customers.

Having grown up at Willesden, on the Bakerloo Line, he moved further out that same route to Stanmore, which he and his wife, son and daughter call home. With that gambling interest, he shaped his week more or less so that he could keep a regular weekly date with his poker school in London. The stakes were not massive.

But once a year he headed off for more serious poker business in Las Vegas, when he still kept a rein on his finances, gambling with thousands rather than tens of thousands. Even when Frank Sinatra was in town, or Tony Bennett or Barbra Streisand, he would see none of them. Like many another regular visitor to Vegas, he was there for the poker.

From lowly days as a clerk at the Mostyn Hotel in London, earning his £17 a week, David Michels had carved an impressive career for himself. By the 1990s he was drawing £300,000 a year as chief executive of Stakis plc. But working seventy or eighty hours a week, he made no apology for that kind of salary, considering his vast responsibilities and the amount he paid in tax.

The further incentive of such people, however, lies in share options which depended on the quality of the man's own performance. That gave him the potential of millionaire status which, as events turned out, would become a reality sooner than anyone expected.

37

SIR LEWIS MAKES WAY

So whatever came of the lofty Sir Lewis Robertson? The bargain he drove on taking on the chairmanship in 1991 included a salary of £120,000 a year, plus 850,000 share options. He remained in the Stakis chair until 1995.

Leaving the management of his own investments to others, his practice had always been to buy 10,000 shares in any company with which he was associated. The shares were in the custody of a fund manager and, on leaving that company, he embargoed any movement for a year, after which his manager could treat them as normal investments. This was to avoid any suspicion of insider dealing.

There would always be something to take up his attention. In 1997 he reached the age of seventy-five but was still battering away at his computer in that quiet corner of Edinburgh. His main interest by then was his role as treasurer to the Royal Society of Edinburgh, a very active scientific, academic and humanitarian group which acts as a kind of think-tank.

Looking back on the Stakis experience, he said: "I admired Sir Reo's resilience tremendously. He had seen what looked like an unassailable empire crumbling away, with one son removed and another son in financial difficulties. Yet he never looked like a man who was bearing such troubles.

"If the banks had firmed up and said they were calling in their money, Stakis would have had to be refinanced on disadvantaged terms, the equity could have been wiped out almost entirely and they would have had to sell urgently at poor prices. It would have been a bad business."

Sir Lewis believed, no doubt with justification, that his own prestige and high reputation with the banks saved the Stakis organisation from such an unthinkable fate. Support for that self-assessment came on the day when, by coincidence, he and Sir Charles Fraser and George Mathewson were all to receive honorary degrees from Edinburgh's Napier University at the same graduation ceremony. Sir Lewis was described as Scotland's best-organised businessman. To that, Sir Charles added: "He is cold and clinical and gives tremendous attention to detail. But I like him."

Sir Lewis's opinion of himself also gained support from the chairman of the Royal Bank of Scotland, Lord Younger (the former George Younger, Secretary of State for Scotland) who encountered the tail-end of the Stakis saga. He said: "As soon as I joined the bank I became fully aware of the situation and we were desperately keen to help the organisation through its problems.

"Too many things had been tried at once and we knew that the prudence of Sir Reo didn't match with running around to get the lowest rates from more than twenty banks. He would never have done that. In the end, it was touch and go—and we got through it by a whisker."

Lord Younger had known Sir Lewis from his days at the Scottish Development Agency and acknowledged that his presence at Stakis had been a source of great confidence at the Royal Bank. As to the credit for the company's salvation, however, he was inclined to spread it more evenly. "It was the skill of Sir Lewis and the integrity of Sir Reo that saved the day," was his conclusion.

Once the ship had steadied course, Sir Lewis was followed into the chair by Richard Cole-Hamilton, a former officer in the Argyll and Sutherland Highlanders, who moved from the family firm of chartered accountants to a career with the Clydesdale Bank, where he became chief executive in 1982.

He in turn stepped aside in the autumn of 1998 and the new chairman of Stakis was Robert Smith, chief executive of Morgan Grenfell Asset Management. Clarifying his greater identity with the Glasgow base of Stakis, he could tell you that he grew up in the Maryhill district of the city, in the shadow of Partick Thistle's home ground, attended Allan Glen's and had thoughts of teaching English before he acquired a taste for economics and went down the path of accountancy instead.

A distinguished career with the Royal Bank of Scotland and the associated Charterhouse Bank was followed by his move to Morgan Grenfell, where his name was much in the news when he was asked by Deutsch Bank, his parent company, to clear up the highly-publicised mess involving fund manager Peter Young.

He was also instrumental in bringing about the high-profile departure of a very well paid fund manager in the City, Ms Nicola Horlick. That incident brought a flock of reporters to the family doorstep, a considerable journey for some, since the Smiths had built a home in the Scottish Borders, near Peebles.

Robert Smith and his wife Alison had by then confirmed that, whatever the demands of his time in London, their preference was always for a life in the country.

38

ANDROS: MY MISTAKES

Whatever his father's private anguish, the most obvious victim of upheaval in the company was Andros Stakis. Sacked and removed in one fell swoop by the incoming Lewis Robertson, he withdrew like a wounded animal to soothe his sores and to consider where it had all gone wrong.

Despite the charges of brashness and arrogance, he was a more sensitive young man than might have been imagined and, as he withdrew to his stately home on the outskirts of Kilbarchan, he entered a period of distress and depression which lasted for several years.

Out on his neck, he had set off on a trip round the world with his journalist wife Barbara, hoping to distance himself from the recent past. But luck was not running his way. Assuming the role of chief executive, in an air of mounting pressure and tension, had coincided with the early days of his marriage and the prevailing atmosphere was hardly conducive to domestic bliss.

That marriage was already running into trouble and when they came back from the world trip, Barbara divorced him. Andros's devastation was complete. He had never wanted her to give up journalism but appreciated the difficulty of retaining that journalistic profile in tandem with her role as Mrs Stakis. Marriage to Andros had inevitably brought her the kind of public attention which she, as a journalist, would have been giving to any other young woman in that position.

He never forgot her words when the business was running into trouble. "Andros, how could you lose so many millions?" she asked ingenuously. It was a long story.

At least there were no children and, after divorce, Barbara was able to resume her career, moving to London to work for the *Evening Standard* and thereafter heading for the United States to run the paper's New York bureau. They remained on amicable terms and Andros never failed to express his deep admiration for Barbara's journalism.

Of course, the same Fourth Estate did not miss a chance to crucify Andros for his contribution to the downfall of his father's company. With a sense of humiliation, he withdrew from the public scene in a welter of self-pity, contemplating that, in record time, he had gone from being a multi-millionaire to a state of financial and emotional crisis. One moment he was the son of one of the richest businessmen in Britain; the next he felt more like a pauper.

In time he could say: "I had four difficult years, both of financial strain and of feeling sorry for myself, but I knew that self-pity was not a good emotion. The experience opened my eyes to many things and gradually my whole life began to change."

In his solitude, he took up hill-walking and found great peace and joy in this pastime. Music became another balm to his broken life as he took lessons and found solace in sitting down at the grand piano in his spacious drawing-room and immersing himself in Chopin. He was turning more and more to his 200-acre estate of Glentyan, on the edge of that weavers' village of Kilbarchan, enjoying his rhododendrons and knowing that he would yet devote more time to the woodlands of his vast acreage.

After several years he began to emerge on the business scene once more, involved with two separate companies, one called

Printhaus and the other one Artlite, which dealt in new-style lighting. Spending much of his time in London, he claimed to be working harder than ever—and for less money.

"But I am not into empire-building," he said emphatically. "I certainly want to make money but this time with a view to enjoying life, as opposed to building a business for the sake of it."

Looking back, he said: "I certainly wish I had done things differently. Where I failed was in not showing myself to be a good listener. Since then I have worked at trying to understand people and their predicaments, to see how they deal with problems and to try to motivate them more.

"I think I have matured and, if I had stayed on, I believe I would have weathered the storm and become an able leader of Stakis. I had put all my money into the company and suddenly I was not in control of the future. It was helmless and nobody seemed to care. I saw Lewis Robertson selling things off while he had no idea of the value of the assets. By dismissing David Aspin, he had nobody left who knew the property side and I reckon that cost the company many millions."

A clever young man, Aspin had been perceived to exert a lot of influence over Andros. Others within the company were wary of his power and some felt he had aspirations to become chief executive himself. After his sacking, he went back south to Kent where he re-entered the property scene, apparently with much success.

Personally, Andros had put his money where his mouth was, except that it was borrowed money which was used for buying more shares in Stakis. When the shares dropped to their lowest, the bank called in his loan and he was in trouble. He did manage to retain some of his holding, however, and partially recovered his position when the share price rose. By the late 1990s, in fact, he was back on the borderline of being a millionaire.

On the subject of his father, his assessment was that Reo had been too much bound up in business, with shooting as his only other interest and not enough time left for communicating with his family.

"Yet I cannot imagine life without him," he said. "We are bound in spirit. Among qualities I have not seen so clearly in any other man, I would dearly love to be at one with his humility. I don't think of him as a businessman but as a wonderful and gentle father. There is something spiritual in it. He has an incredibly steadying power, as if God is testing him.

"His greatest strength is that, when you are in crisis, he becomes an amazingly supportive man. He finds the compassion and is there when you need him. You just wonder why it takes a crisis to make him like this."

The adoration is nevertheless against a background of frequent conflict between the two. He remembers stalking into his father's office one day to complain that he was backing the other directors at the expense of his own son. Rather losing the place, he shouted: "You have never supported me!" And he walked out, slamming the door behind him.

Sir Reo followed him through to concede the point, but quietly reminded Andros that, whatever else you do, you don't slam doors like that. Andros never forgot the lesson.

There was another brief statement which would stick in his memory: "Andros, I had no problems until you came along." Yet he is the first to point out that his father has been overwhelmingly the most important influence on his life.

Andros may not be building empires any more but, for all the ups and downs, Sir Reo continued to believe that his elder son would yet emerge as an important figure in the business world. That supportive quality of the parents comes through again and again in the testimony of the family. From the distance of their homes in Athens, Limassol and Los Angeles, the Stakis girls had for long kept an almost daily contact with their mother, Annitsa, and knew that, in the moment of business crisis, she was the solid rock of support, exactly the force Sir Reo needed at his side.

At her home in Cyprus, Niki continued to marvel at the strength which made her parents such a wonderful couple. Her father was always the friend to whom she could talk in a moment of personal crisis and he could handle such a situation with remarkable aplomb. Among the lessons he taught her was how to be discreet.

She had to find out for herself the extent of his charity work, about which he had said nothing. It emerged that no-one in Cyprus had ever asked for help and not received it. Whether gift or loan, he took the attitude that people had given him such help in his own early life that he should do the same for others.

Even at the height of his own troubles in 1990, she discovered, he was helping others when there was more than enough to concern him at home. "How can you fail to learn from a man like that?" she asked. She reckoned it came from a strong faith, a sense of which she tries to pass on to her own children, though she is not the church-goer that her parents have been.

Sir Reo's generosity was known to two other people in particular. Discreet in the best traditions of her profession, Frances Timoney would keep the information to herself. But, as the boss's secretary, she would gulp nevertheless at the cheques she was writing out on behalf of the Reo Stakis Charitable Foundation. They would run into tens of thousands at a time.

As the PR boss, Alex Pagett might respect the man's modesty but he could hardly believe that such vast sums were being disbursed in total privacy, without one iota of publicity being gained in return. With the arrival of David Michels as chief executive, the staff became more closely associated with the raising of funds for charity.

Coming to terms with the scale of her father's generosity, daughter Niki appreciated the fact that the Stakis family were a vibrant, close-knit unit who would rush to support each other when the chips were down. And she made two significant points which were basic to the raison d'être of this book. She believed it was important for the family to realise that their father made mistakes in life—and that you must learn from such mistakes. But there was an even more important lesson to be learned. And it was that, even when you make your mistakes, it is not the end of the world.

39

THE MEMORY OF DUNBLANE

Understandably, the troubles at Stakis were a source of deep hurt and humiliation to Sir Reo, the man who had formed his own company as far back as the war and had guided it for nearly fifty years with phenomenal success.

To reach the heights of a merchant prince, lauded and fêted wherever he went, only to see his whole business creation slip away from his grasp, was a bitter blow which only a man of deep inner strength could have absorbed with dignity.

Archbishop Gregorios observed events from the distance of London and said: "He had the faith and richness of character which enabled him to endure his misfortunes. He managed to remain calm and to keep a faith in man's future and in God's providence."

For Sir Reo had not only been obliged to step aside, taking on an honorary role of president and non-executive director, but he had witnessed his beloved son sacked by his successor, Sir Lewis Robertson, and despatched to years of devastation.

It may not have been a matter of material importance but one of the most wounding incidents during the crisis and reorganisation of the business came when Sir Lewis refused to give Sir Reo an office at the new headquarters of Stakis in Atlantic Quay, Glasgow.

Sir Reo felt it a matter of principle that he should be given better treatment than this and fought hard to keep a toe-hold at the company HQ. Sir Lewis was no doubt trying to keep him at a distance from the executives, fearing that proximity might tempt interference, but you cannot help feeling that a touch of psychology, not to mention a hint of humanity, might have led to a compromise.

But hard as Sir Reo fought, he lost that battle and realised he had not even a cubby-hole within the Stakis empire to call his own. It was something he found hard to swallow. There was, of course, still a role for the founder within the organisation. As president, he would be attending board meetings every month and his contract stipulated that he would remain with the company until his 90th birthday, which would fall on 13th March in the year 2003.

He would still serve on committees within the company and time would show that, as always in the past, no opening of a new hotel would be complete without his presence. As a proven expert in the conduct of hotels, he continued to visit those establishments and to give discreet hints to the management if he noticed anything requiring attention.

Because of a long-standing loyalty and the high calibre of staff, there was not much to complain about. Such loyalty was rewarded twice a year, at ceremonies in East Kilbride and Bradford, when bonuses were distributed, and Sir Reo never failed to highlight the part that employees had played in maintaining the profits of the company. Such involvement of staff was just one of the ways in which he had for long shown himself to be ahead of his time.

Without a working base, Sir Reo had to settle for his own home, or rather the two homes which had served the family since he introduced his bride from Cyprus at the end of the Second World War. That villa in Aytoun Road, Pollokshields, in one of Glasgow's more exclusive quarters, had remained the Stakis family home until 1985. With six lively children, the space had been less than completely adequate and there was talk of building a bigger house.

Sir Reo had a better idea, however, which brought him face to face with another of life's uncanny coincidences. With thoughts of buying a country estate, he was scanning the newspapers one day when he noticed a desirable property on the market. It was called Glentyan House at Kilbarchan.

Glentyan House? It had a familiar ring. Wasn't that the mansion where the man had turned him away all those years ago—with the lace which had been ordered by his wife? Reo sent his lawyer to negotiate a successful deal on his behalf and, in due course, the family was waiting to greet the new owner of the house.

When he eventually turned up, the chap who stepped out of the Rolls-Royce, they discovered, was none other than the familiar little fellow from Cyprus! Before entering the house, however, he would have to fetch something from the car. It was a bundle of lace which had been ordered for this mansion many years ago and would now find its proper place after all.

Reo Stakis would see that his dear mother's work had not been in vain—and the 200 acres of Glentyan remain in the Stakis family to this day.

As it happened, the children were growing up and away, and Annitsa decided she would be too lonely there, leaving the spacious mansion to become the home of Andros.

Sir Reo had another thought. On buying Dunblane Hydro in 1962, he had acquired a modest house on an adjacent site, which had been used by the previous owner of the hotel. It became a holiday home for the Stakis clan but in the 1980s he had a plan which he managed to keep a secret from his wife. Using that house as a nucleus, he enlarged it into a splendid ranch-type home.

Lady Stakis knew nothing about it until they drove out casually to Dunblane one day in 1984—and she couldn't believe what had happened to the place. It was love at first sight and within months she had left her city home for good and taken up residence in the peace and fresh air of the Perthshire countryside.

The Aytoun Road villa was Sir Reo's private property and became the work-base of his secretary, Frances Timoney, when there was no office to go to. She would ply between there and Dunblane to maintain the flow of her secretarial work. From her earliest days in the 1960s, she had found herself doubling as secretary and chauffeur, thrown in at the deep end of the automobile experience by driving once round the block to acquaint herself with the faint purr of the Rolls-Royce!

Thereafter, it would be the regular morning task to collect her boss at Aytoun Road and drive him to company headquarters in the city centre, having become master of that Rolls (or four of the exquisite creatures, to be exact) which would be her daily mode of transport for decades to come. At first it would raise the eyebrows of curious neighbours to find such a vehicle parked outside her own home in the west end of Glasgow.

Now the routine was quite different, with regular runs to that Stakis home set discreetly in the trees, within a short walk of Dunblane Hydro. There she would deliver her latest secretarial offerings and take instructions for the next.

Dunblane was one of Scotland's most desirable little communities, rescued from being a traffic bottleneck on the main route from Glasgow to Perth when it was bypassed by a motorway and left in the peace which its picturesque setting deserved.

It was one of the weird ironies of our time that such an idyllic corner of a civilised country should be chosen by the fates for one of mankind's most unthinkable atrocities. As usual, Sir Reo was up early that morning of 13th March, 1996, contemplating that this was his eighty-third birthday and that, later in the day, family and friends would be gathering for a small celebration at Dunblane Hydro.

His personal lawyer, David MacRobert from Glasgow, had been on business up north and remembered that he must call on Sir Reo on the way south. There was something which needed a signature. Coming out of the hills, he had not caught up with the news bulletins and arrived at the Stakis home in fine fettle, only to find his client in a state of dejection.

Hadn't he heard the news? That morning, a dubious and troubled character called Thomas Hamilton, who ran boys' clubs in the district and had a grudge against society, waved cheerily to his neighbour in the nearby town of Stirling and boarded a bus for Dunblane, contemplating the heinous crime he was about to commit.

Soon after the children of Dunblane School had skipped inside for their day's lessons, this fiendish creature burst into the gymnasium and confronted a classful of five-year-olds with his guns a-blazing. Within minutes, sixteen of those children, along with their teacher, lay dead or dying in a nightmare scenario which would imprint itself on world consciousness in much the same way as we remembered what we were doing when President Kennedy was shot in 1963.

Having completed his evil mission, Thomas Hamilton then turned the gun on himself, no doubt having satisfied some deranged ambition to go out in a blaze of suicidal notoriety. His single act put the name of Dunblane into the vocabulary of those who would never have heard of it, as a symbol of much that was sick in our so-called civilised society. It led to a successful campaign for the banning of most guns in the United Kingdom, not that anything was likely to have prevented a madman like Hamilton from acquiring the weapons of his evil intent.

Ironically, the reason why Sir Reo's lawyer was calling that afternoon was to secure his signature for the renewal of his gun licence, the sport of shooting on the moors of Scotland being his only relaxation from the pressures of business. Needless to say, he had no stomach for such thoughts that ghastly day. Instead, having cancelled his birthday celebration, he offered Dunblane Hydro for whatever purpose it could suitably be used.

With its services for the victims of the massacre, Dunblane Cathedral, part of the Church of Scotland, became a familiar sight on television screens all over the world. Long before that, Sir Reo and Lady Stakis could be found worshipping there, when they were not at their own Greek Orthodox Cathedral in Glasgow. Sir Reo had for long pointed to the similarity between the Scots and the Cypriots who were, after all, both plain, hard-working folk and all part of the Christian community.

If the wider world had to familiarise itself with the name of Dunblane, there was one small corner of the Mediterranean where no such need existed. On the island of Cyprus the good folk of Kato-Drys knew instantly that it was the home of their favourite son, the benefactor who had done so much for their primitive village, bringing them water and electricity and so much else.

They responded as well as they could, offering the balm of their Mediterranean sunshine if it would help other children from Dunblane to spend a holiday on their idyllic island.

40

CHAMPAGNE WITH CHIPS?

The long-standing traditions of business, in Britain as well as Greece, might not have accommodated the idea but it is interesting to speculate on what might have happened if Sir Reo's daughter Rena had had her way.

Her desire for women's rights, expressed mainly in her opposition to arranged marriages, could very easily extend to business succession. The thought is unlikely to have entered her father's head but if he had not been so focused on the career of son Andros, he might have found a successor in one of his daughters. Who knows?

It has happened to at least one other prominent Scottish businessman, Gordon Baxter of Fochabers, whose famous food-canning firm came under the command of daughter Audrey in preference to one of his sons.

Sir Reo's daughter Rena is one who regrets that she could not have been treated as an equal: "I would like to have been at Dad's right hand in business. There is more to me than he might have thought and, if times had been different, I feel I could have been on the board of Stakis."

Within most of Sir Reo's children lie traces of his own drive and ambition, whatever has been passed on in the way of wisdom and good judgement. Indeed it would be strange if the genes had not performed in this way.

Alex Pagett is just one among thousands who marvel at the combination of qualities which enabled Sir Reo to build the Stakis empire with such sure-footed confidence and success. Invited out to lunch one day, Pagett had first-hand experience of the meticulous care he could take, not least in studying what the opposition might be up to.

Pagett had no idea of the destination until he was comfortably seated in the taxi and was given the hint that they were going for fish and chips. But this would be no ordinary fish supper. Harry Ramsden had just opened up in Glasgow and a little friendly espionage was called for.

Sir Reo was no sooner inside the distinctive edifice on the south side of the Clyde, near the Kingston Bridge, than he went fairly blatantly on a tour of inspection. What was this person doing? What was that for? Once they had sat down, he called for champagne. The young Glasgow waiter was taken aback. They didn't really serve champagne with fish and chips. No champagne? Well, what else was there? Alex Pagett intervened to say he would happily settle for a beer. The waiter was happy too.

When the Scottish Council held a forum at Aviemore, Alex Pagett thought the company should lay on a reception for the movers and shakers who would be there. When Sir Reo turned up he was appalled to find they were being offered a selection of drinks. He summoned the managing director of hotels. On a prestigious occasion like this, the drink on offer should have been nothing but champagne.

Said Pagett: "He has a gut feeling for what is right and what is wrong. And he has been far ahead of his time, which you realise when you hear business philosophies being discussed today. Companies talk about listening to what the customer has to say. Reo Stakis was doing that thirty years ago.

"They say you must have quality control, you must be consistent—and you must give value for money. He was putting all that into practice thirty years ago. He would look at the company butcher's bill and decide it would be better to buy a farm, responsible for raising their own beef cattle.

"He wasn't making speeches or writing books about it. He simply did it. Above all, I realised he was kindness itself, instilling a lot of enthusiasm in people."

When Sir Reo stood down as chairman, Pagett suggested a dinner in his honour and turned his mind to an appropriate gift to mark the occasion, which would be held at the Dunkeld House Hotel. In discussion with an artist in Perth, he settled on a silver quaich but struck on the further idea of giving it a base from the olive trees of Cyprus. So it was that the two countries closest to his heart came together in a splendid symbol of his life—and there have been few moments when he was so deeply moved.

When he became less involved in the affairs of the company, he still attended board meetings and was on the phone on a regular basis, wanting to know how things were going. Was everybody happy? It was simply in the nature of the man.

He gained a new lease of life with a heart bypass operation in 1995. It cast some light on the philosophy of the man when, on the eve of that operation, he told Sir Charles Fraser: "I was in church on Sunday and it occurred to me I should pray that the operation would go well. But then I thought you should pray only for that which you deserve. And at eighty-two I'm not sure I deserve more good health."

41

RETURN TO CYPRUS

In the springtime of 1998, Reo Stakis was back in Kato-Drys, the village which reared him and to which he bade farewell that day more than seventy years earlier when he set out for the distant shores of Great Britain, still short of his fifteenth birthday.

Now he was back among the ghosts of another age, wandering with his private thoughts and memories and pausing by the corner grocery which served the whole community and which, with his impish sense of humour, he liked to call "the Sainsbury's of Kato-Drys." There was never any need for a bakery in the village since the women all baked their own bread anyway.

He dallied again by his old school, now boarded up and no longer needed in the modern context, and began to recite the names of boys who had been his friends in those far-off days. How easily they came back to his mind, names like Haris Charalambous, Panagis Perdikou, Solomos Hadgioannou, Nick Koutsakos, Michael Perados, Stavrinos Panagi, Savas Panagi and Zenon Perdikou.

Some of them were no longer with us but the sadness of that thought soon gave way to the surprise of running into another old classmate, Angelis Solomon, the one who recalled the teacher's prophesy that that little boy (Reo Stakis) would one day be a great man.

Angelis was another reminder that, for all the rustic and paro-

239

chial nature of those Cypriot villages, there was also a cosmopolitan side to their tradition. While we rightly marvel at the adventure of a fourteen-year-old Reo Stakis setting out for Britain, it was not a unique happening in the context of Cypriot society.

Just as many a small nation, or grouping like the Western Isles of Scotland, sent mariners to the far ends of the earth in numbers out of all proportion to their size, so has Cyprus despatched its young men to sell lace and other commodities, the principal destinations being Britain and the United States.

In the case of Angelis Solomon, he began by pursuing a route similar to that of Reo Stakis, arriving in Britain a year later and teaming up with his old classmate, sometimes travelling on the back of his motorbike but quite soon coming to the conclusion that door-to-door selling was not in his nature.

Whereas the more doughty Stakis could take the rebuffs and bounce back with a better way of selling his goods, Angelis found it hard to cope with a door being closed on his face. By 1930 he had given up selling lace in Britain and set out for America, switching to that other profession for which people of Greek origin are well-known.

Much earlier than Reo, Angelis found his way into the hotel and restaurant business, albeit as a porter and working his way through to waiter in the Fifth Avenue Hotel, which was second only to the Waldorf Astoria on the New York scene. It gave him a privileged view of the glamorous world of showbusiness in the 1930s, when the clientele would include film stars like Bette Davis and composers like Irving Berlin.

But it was not all glamour in the United States. The great Depression had struck and times were hard for most people. Angelis decided it was time to go back home to Cyprus, where he remained from 1938 until after the Second World War. But the wanderlust was still with him and he decided to give Britain a second chance. This time he headed for Manchester and, with a wealth of experience behind him, began to establish a prosperous restaurant business, making himself a good living, as reflected in the fashionable surroundings of Wilmslow, which he called home.

Only when he was seventy-four did he sell up his business and, leaving children and grandchildren in his adopted land, make his way back to Cyprus and to Kato-Drys, where he would live out the rest of his days.

To the modern visitor it may seem that villages like these had been caught in a time warp, unchanged from ancient days, yet to people like Reo and Angelis they were vastly different from what they remembered. The quiet grind of rural industry and the chatter of a larger population were gone.

Reo stopped by a derelict little house and remembered that that was once the home of the priest who was his grandfather, now overgrown and symbolic of so much that had happened to Kato-Drys. The houses which had survived were now more often holiday homes or belonged to people like Angelis, back from their foreign adventures to spend their eventide in Cyprus.

But the focus of this particular day lay up the hill at a modern restaurant which commanded a breathtaking view of the valley below. It was here they were gathering for a lunch which would bring together so many of the family and friends of Reo Stakis. A famous son had come home and the lunch would be spent with people who spoke his native language and shared a culture in much the same spirit as you would find in many a remote corner of Scotland.

They brought in the food and wine in abundance and the babble of animated conversation was ample proof of a joyous occasion, natural and uninhibited, where everybody was completely at home and enjoying it.

It was some measure of the standing of Sir Reo on his native island that the country's Minister of Justice dropped by for lunch. So did the recent Ambassador to London. Everyone knew that Reo was back on the island and they all wanted to pay their respects. Some had never left Kato-Drys but among those exiles who had come back for good was another familiar face from the Glasgow scene. Zenon Perdikou used to own the Stockwell Restaurant in Stockwell Street.

The buzz of conversation lasted through the afternoon till the party broke up and began to wend its way down to the heart of the village. Among those with tales to tell had been Peter Petropoulos, a cousin of Lady Stakis, who had also followed the trail to Britain in 1935, trained in mining and returned to become an expert back home.

He was recalling the day war broke out in 1939 and how he joined the congregation at the Greek Orthodox Church in central London. Prime Minister Neville Chamberlain had announced the British ultimatum to Hitler to suspend his invasion of Poland. In the absence of a response that Sunday morning of 3rd September, we were at war with Germany as from 11am.

Peter Petropoulos recalled the atmosphere in the Greek Church as the bells chimed out eleven—and women started screaming. Their belief that the Germans would start bombing London immediately was strengthened by an air-raid siren which began to wail across the capital. As it happened, it was a false alarm, sparked off by an aeroplane approaching the south coast of England and being mistakenly identified as German. Memories, memories.

Reo Stakis bade farewell to old friends, cast a nostalgic look around the scene of his childhood and drove off down the valley towards the monastery which held vigil on the slopes below. There, once again, he was greeted joyously by nuns, several of whom were of Kato-Drys background and with whom he drank home-made lemon juice, the health-giving additive which adorned his every meal.

Back in Limassol that evening there was time to reflect on the day's events over dinner and to plan where he would go next morning. This was a poignant stage in the history of Cyprus. An island divided by the conflicting interests of Greeks and Turks was seeking its way into the European Community. Crucial negotiations were due in the autumn of 1998, not that the conflict itself could be resolved in that short time.

But the Americans and Russians were seeking to influence events, President Clinton's special envoy, Richard Holbrooke, and a Russian envoy arriving on the island during Reo Stakis's visit. It was a busy time for the President of Cyprus, 79-year-old Glafcos Clerides, too busy perhaps for him to see one of his island's most famous sons. A phone-call would determine the matter one way or another.

42

A PRESIDENT'S WELCOME

Whatever the affairs of state, President Clerides had cleared the decks to meet Reo Stakis on his nostalgic return to Cyprus. This famous son had known the President's father, as well as himself, and the pressing schedule of appointments with visiting envoys and ambassadors was rearranged to accommodate the man from Scotland who had done so much for his homeland of Cyprus.

The limousine which took Sir Reo up the driveway of the spacious grounds would stop by the portico of the Presidential Palace, where a military band was already in position to play the national anthems of visiting dignitaries.

This was not the first time Sir Reo had been in these impressive surroundings, his visits dating back to the days of the British Governor, when his contacts in the United Kingdom gave him an entrée to high places on his native island. A short wait in the anteroom, facing out to the magnificent gardens of the palace, was followed by a minor flurry of flunkeys as he was escorted to the President's private room, where the two men embraced in remembrance of previous family contact.

Clerides, a rotund and jolly figure of smallish stature, had become widely known not only for his statesmanlike endeavours but for his explosive sense of humour. His storytelling was legendary and at that moment of much publicity about the private life of President Clinton, he had his own contribution to offer on the humorous side of events, one to which even the man in the White House himself would not have objected!

Had Sir Reo heard the one about the new Pope being briefed on the protocol of receiving VIPs in the aftermath of his installation? First he would meet the cardinals, then the ambassadors to the Vatican and finally the rabbi, who would bear a brown envelope. But the Pope was not expected to ask what the envelope contained. At the last minute, however, he could not resist the temptation.

"What's in the envelope?" asked the Pontiff.

"The bill for the Last Supper!" replied the rabbi.

President Clerides offered current stories against himself, fully establishing the terms of familiarity and good humour on which the audience would be conducted. Reo Stakis was much at home with his fellow-Cypriot, whose credentials were impressive to say the least.

Born in Nicosia in 1919, he had volunteered for the Royal Air Force in 1939, heading for Lossiemouth, on the Moray Firth of Scotland, to undergo his training as a bomber pilot. From Wellingtons to Lancasters, he was soon ready for active service but in 1942 his plane was shot down over Germany and he was taken to the prisoner-of-war camp at Lamsdorf.

From there he escaped and after recapture escaped again, a daring adventure from which he was lucky to get away with his life. In recollection of that experience, he was showing Sir Reo the position of his wrists when the Germans proceeded to put him in chains for a whole year thereafter.

After the war he studied law at King's College, London University, and in 1951 was called to the Bar at Gray's Inn Road. From then until 1960 he practised in Cyprus but within that period he was serving, this time against the British, with the EOKA fighters in the struggle for independence. As a lawyer, he defended several of his comrades who had been arrested by the British.

After four years of guerrilla warfare in the Troodos Mountains, when the name of the EOKA founder and leader, Colonel George Grivas, was seldom out of the news, Cyprus finally gained its independence in 1960, when Archbishop Makarios, who had collaborated with the anti-British forces, became the first President, as part of that Byzantine tradition where church and state were intertwined. However, it was the last time this would happen.

But Makarios would soon run into his own troubles as head of state, when the group of colonels grabbed dictatorial power in Greece in 1967 and set their sights on annexing Cyprus as part of their own country. To that end, the military junta backed an attempt to overthrow Makarios in July, 1974, causing the Archbishop to flee into exile, during which time Glafcos Clerides temporarily assumed the duties of President until Makarios managed to return in December of that year.

The outcome of the coup was that Turkey, in the ongoing conflict with its Greek neighbours, took the opportunity to invade Cyprus, ostensibly to protect the interests of the Turkish minority but in effect to establish a claim to the northern part of the island. Despite the protests of the United Nations and others, that powerful army of 35,000 men was still there quarter of a century later, answering to its own leader, Mr Rauf Denktash, and not to the official government of the Cyprus state, headed by President Clerides.

Such was the ongoing dilemma of the President as he entered his second term of office in 1998, which would take him through to 2003, when he would have reached the age of eighty-four.

Ironically, President Clerides and his Turkish rival had been law students together in London after the war and were on familiar terms as human beings. As politicians, they were sparring partners in a deadlock which divided Cyprus in two, the respective leaders facing each other across a "Berlin Wall" which separated north from south, even running across residential streets in the capital of Nicosia.

Despite the handicap, Clerides pursued the objective of taking Cyprus into the European Union, even if Mr Denktash and his community were refusing to have anything to do with it until their own domestic situation was resolved. As a hint of the personal pride and animosity involved, the Turkish leader complained that he had wasted years on inter-communal talks through the United Nations but "when we walk out of the room he is President Clerides and I am just Mr Denktash."

With such burdens of state on his shoulders, the President's keen sense of humour could perhaps be seen as a safety valve for the frustrations besetting his attempts to bring a lasting peace to Cyprus.

In this private audience with the President, Reo Stakis had the privilege of hearing from the man himself about the strategy of taking Cyprus into Europe. He acknowledged that the Greeks and Turks shared a fear that each would be overrun by the other; but he was pursuing that entry to the EU in the belief that it would be the best safeguard for both communities. As part of the Union, neither would be able to do what the other feared.

He recognised that he was taking a gamble, which could be a catalyst for better or worse, with the chance of either ending the division of the island or exacerbating the problem. But he reckoned it was a gamble worth taking.

Reo Stakis bade the President farewell and considered that, if a sense of humour had anything to with it, then Clerides was the best hope for finding a solution. As he drove back into the city of Nicosia, passing the bullet-ridden hotel where he used to stay when visiting the capital, he viewed the sentry-posts and their armed guards with an unspeakable sadness. Along that border there were posters on the walls, proclaiming atrocities in graphic detail, again not dissimilar from scenes in Northern Ireland.

Sir Reo could only repair to a street café, order lunch and a glass of wine and ponder what had happened to his beloved island that it could tear itself apart in such racial division. He remembered times gone by when Turkish women were among those who brought back the lace to his mother's courtyard in Kato-Drys. They were all friends and neighbours who sat down together at the end of the day and enjoyed a camaraderie of mutual respect.

The news of a conclusion to peace talks on Northern Ireland was coming across on the radio that day, hailed as a major break-through at least on the surface, whatever the final outcome of that conflict might be.

So far, there was no such chink of hope for Cyprus. But that would be foremost in his thoughts and prayers as he took his farewells of family and friends and headed for Larnaca Airport at the end of a poignant visit to the land of his birth.

As Sir Reo prepared to board the plane for Glasgow, he took one last look at this island in the sun and remembered a decision he had made a long time ago. For all his love of Scotland, his deep commitment to the adopted land and his firm conviction that it was home, he had made provision that his remains at the end of the day would be brought back here to Cyprus, to the soil of his seeding.

A late burst of unseasonable snow in April awaited him as his plane touched down at Glasgow Airport. Little did he know that, within a short time, that vast empire he had built during the past 50 years would be swallowed up in the name of Hilton International.

His own proud name of Stakis, which had found its way into the vocabulary of his adopted country as a symbol of good eating, would step into the shadow of a mighty rival.

From its beginnings in that little village in Cyprus, the story of Reo Stakis had been akin to a fairy-tale, mainly of triumphant success. But through all the toil and sweat of building the Stakis organisation, this final denouement was not the one he would have chosen for his ultimate reward. At the age of eighty-six, he did not expect to be coping with what was nothing short of a heartbreak.

Business wisdom, they said, had dictated the inevitable. But for Reo Stakis, on that February day of 1999 when he said farewell to his shareholders and friends at Dunblane Hydro, it was time to shed a private tear. As befitted a man of great dignity and generous spirit, he did so with decorum—and just the hint of a brave and gracious smile.

INDEX